ARADALE

THE MAKING OF A HAUNTED ASYLUM

ARADALE

THE MAKING OF A HAUNTED ASYLUM

DAVID WALDRON, SHARN WALDRON &
NATHANIEL BUCHANAN

ARCADIA

With thanks to

Bruce Waldron for editing

The Support of Eerie Tours

The remarkable building complex of the former
Ararat Mental Hospital

First published 2020 by ARCADIA
the general books' imprint of
Australian Scholarly Publishing Pty Ltd
7 Lt Lothian St Nth, North Melbourne, Vic 3051
Tel: 03 9329 6963 / Fax: 03 9329 5452
enquiry@scholarly.info / www.scholarly.info

ISBN 978-1-925984-91-0

Cover design: Wayne Saunders

Cover: Ararat Asylum Tours, 2015. Courtesy Eerie Tours

Contents

INTRODUCTION

Exploring the 'Haunted Asylum'

> The Aradale Lunatic Asylum housed my intellectually disabled brother for ten days during the 1960s. Although this time was brief, his experience there was horrendous. It has become a traumatic moment that stays with me to this day.
>
> Today this old former Lunatic Asylum, an institution of the Victorian era, has become a tourist attraction. Aradale, in Ararat, runs ghost tours through the old asylum that only closed in the early 1990s. So, what are people drawn to? Is it the stories the guides tell them, the display of artefacts of violence, or imagining the imbeciles who were once housed there? (Dickson, 2013, 10)

If you approach the regional Victorian town of Ararat your eye is invariably drawn to the rather ominous looking nineteenth century towers rising above the tree line on a tall isolated hill on the outskirts of town. As the regional centre of Ararat comes into view, there is an A frame sign identifying an innocuous small country road as the path to the Ararat Mental Hospital and Aradale Ghost Tours. If you choose to follow this road a curious visitor is greeted by the once beautiful, but now decrepit and overgrown, Italianate gatehouse, serving as the solitary guardian of what lies beyond. Continuing along the road which soon ascends a hill densely enclosed on all sides by trees, the visitor is suddenly struck by the enormous and imposing façade of Aradale (the later informal term for the Ararat Lunatic Asylum), a spectacular Victorian era lunatic asylum still perched on the highest part of this remote, rural Australian town. An old sign, now discoloured and crooked, still attempts to proudly display the asylum's name. The front building itself had always been impressive but now, with its broken windows, peeling paint and cobwebs, it exudes an atmosphere of neglect and dread. Peering through the enormous entrance gates, a visitor can see a vast complex of buildings stretching off into the distance.

The grounds of the former Ararat Lunatic Asylum are, today, a crumbling labyrinth of dozens of abandoned buildings in various states of disrepair. The original design, overseen by public works architect John Clark, was inspired by the Kirkbride Asylum system and modelled on the large Colney Hatch asylum in London. It also featured several new innovations such as large outdoor courtyards for patients to enjoy, 'ha-ha' or sunken walls and an orange gate lodge. Since this time numerous additions, cottages, corridors and facilities have been built onto the complex, creating a bewildering array of architectural styles and complex thoroughfares, a chaotic maze for the contemporary visitor to navigate. Today, the former Ararat Lunatic Asylum/Ararat Mental Hospital/Aradale complex is a major focal point for heritage and tourism. The nearly one hundred and thirty years of patient care, in a sense, provide a window into the history of Australian psychiatric treatment; the buildings are remarkable examples of Victorian Italianate architecture, reminiscent of approaches to the design of Victorian era asylums across the British Empire. As the VHS Heritage listing of the former Ararat asylum comments,

> Aradale is historically and socially important for its physical manifestation of the changing approaches to the treatment of mental illness in Victoria from institutional confinement

> to treatment and rehabilitation, and from barracks, through cottages to wards. Aradale was a key component in a system of nineteenth century asylums which included those at Beechworth and Kew. Aradale has been crucially important in the social history of Ararat and has, along with the Ararat Gaol, contributed significantly to the economic viability and survival of the town. Its size and prominent siting have had an important and long lived social and economic impact on the town and region. (https://vhd.heritagecouncil.vic.gov.au/places/28)

During its period of operation, the building was renamed three times, each name representing a shift in the philosophy of Australian psychiatric care. Initially named the Ararat Lunatic Asylum, it was renamed the Ararat Hospital for the Insane in 1903. From 1933 to 1959 it was officially the Aradale Mental Hospital before finally being renamed, unofficially, the Aradale Psychiatric Hospital in 1962. Since 2008 the site has been utilized by a community organization of former staff, volunteers and their descendants, the Friends of J Ward, associated with the former asylum for the criminally insane, based in Ararat's former Victorian-era goal. More recently the Aradale site has become the home of an extremely successful ghost-tour and haunting industry run by the Ballarat based company Eerie Tours which takes thousands of local and international guests through a variety of dark history and ghost-hunting tours each year.

Mass media and popular representations of the Ararat Lunatic Asylum's history can read much like a gothic horror novel, contributing to public fascination with the site. Horror and the gothic have always held a deep allure for the public, which still resonates to this day. This can be seen in the popularity of films like *Lady in Black*, *Silence of the Lambs* and *The Conjuring*, but it is not just films that are popular; authors like H. P. Lovecraft, Peter Straub, Anne Rice, and Stephen King are famous for their stories of horror and the macabre. The intention of the author is to create feelings of disgust, loathing and terror. Stephen King in his book

Danse Macabre reflects on the appeal of gothic literature and suggests that horror appeals to us because it offers us a chance to encounter emotions and thoughts that would be unacceptable in our society. (King, 1981, 33) But there may be another explanation for the popularity of the macabre; a Jungian psychological approach would understand the horror expressed through Aradale as representing an aspect of the collective shadow. The shadow is a central aspect of analytical psychology. When actions are so bizarrely out of character with what is intended, almost invariably it is indicative that the shadow is at work. For Jung, the shadow is the thing a person has no wish to be, 'the thing he is not, (the other).' (Jung, 1954, para. 470) When a community moves in a certain direction there is always a part of the collective psyche that is left behind and remains undeveloped and childlike; this is what is being described by the term 'The Shadow'. This is true both at personal and communal levels. The shadow aspect of ourselves, like a child, simply reacts and has no capacity for moderated, thoughtful response. If a society adopts as its persona an image of superior, rational, moderated humanity then the shadow, that undeveloped aspect of the collective, will find expression, in this case through senseless brutality, as in the treatment of convicts and Indigenous people from the outset of the convict era, and as in the treatment of people designated as mad. The very existence of these brutalized groups is an indication that much has been consigned to the shadow and so there is a double jeopardy: on one side, the treatment of these inconvenient truths must, of necessity, be hidden because they already participate in that which has been put aside. On the other hand, this lack of attention must also be hidden because it symbolizes that part of the psyche which has been relegated, in Jungian terms, to the shadow, that which is not known. Aradale's history has been beset by scandal, the 'scandalous hidden' intruding horrifyingly into the visible, rational façade, but time and again not finding a lasting resolution.

Throughout this book, there will be frequent references to analytical psychology and its founder, Carl Jung. Analytical psychology is interested in ghosts and ghost stories, not so much about whether ghosts exist or not but rather, who is it that sees ghosts and why? Under what emotional, mental and physical conditions does a person see a ghost, and if they do, what is its meaning; what does it symbolize? For Jung, symbols are a form of language, images that convey a reference and meaning of something else, something significant but hidden or unknown. In this context a symbol has a numinous quality only dimly perceived by the conscious mind. What matters is the reality of the experience. Jungian (analytical) psychology takes ghostly encounters seriously and so there is a deep curiosity as to why visitors to Aradale, a place represented as redolent with horror, violence and death, are drawn to pay money to embark on ghost tours and walk through dilapidated and decaying buildings that once housed individuals designated with what at the time was called madness, in conditions that were often brutal, painful, mentally destructive and emotionally torturous. For Jung, a 'ghostly' experience, whether it is encountered as an event which comes upon a person unbidden and unexpected or through the contrived atmosphere of a ghost tour, is nevertheless an indicator of much deeper stirrings in the psyche of the individual within his or her cultural context. Ghosts, in whatever manifestation they are encountered, are a window into the internal workings of the psyche of the society and the individual.

The shadow is encountered through its projection onto some 'other', and that may be an individual, family, a religious or ethnic grouping, and the shadow is often glimpsed in the way a society treats its most disadvantaged citizens. Throughout history, people designated as mad have been managed through confinement by family members but more recently they have been locked up in prisons and madhouses and confined to large institutions. Often people were designated mad because they did not fit in with what, at the time, were considered to be the social norms of society. Aradale housed some of the most disadvantaged citizens but they were often feared and seen as a threat to the order of society; they confronted the society with its vulnerability to the irrational, the disordered, the unpredictable, society's shadow which it sought so hard to suppress and eradicate.

In this book we will be exploring the creation of a haunted site through its tumultuous one hundred and fifty year history and how an institution built for the most laudable of reasons and best of intentions has come to be viewed as 'Australia's most haunted building'. In it we will journey through the history of Aradale, the changing public perceptions of the building, its patients and its staff as the institution is repeatedly rocked by scandal and reframed through changes in public perceptions of madness and its treatment, and the experiences of the disenfranchised who lived within Aradale's walls. We will explore what has made the site of the former Ararat Lunatic Asylum, in popular imagination, the most haunted site in Australia.

1

The Asylum

> Hospitals are in some sort the measure of the civilization of a people and this sentiment applies in an especial manner to the case of hospitals for the treatment and cure of the insane. A people testifies in the most direct manner to the high tone of its civilization by making full provision for the soothing and curative treatment of the insane. (*Melbourne Leader*, 6.3.1869, 17)

The asylum and its legacy permeates contemporary Australia, especially in communities where, for so long, the asylum was a centre of the town's economy, employment and culture. As Dolly MacKinnon comments,

> Memories of Asylums as places are now all around us; embodied in the empty building structures, in the archives, the oral histories, and the objects and sounds of the past. (MacKinnon, 2002, 5)

The history of the asylum system under discussion is integrally linked with how lunacy has been conceptualized in Australia and much of the western world. The asylum needs to be understood in the context of colonialism and its custodial practices and this context did not end at some point in our history; it is still an active part of our culture, a tradition that runs from the origins of European colonialization to contemporary practices that have instigated Manus Island internment for refugees. Mental illness is not a clear entity, nor is it clear why people need to be incarcerated; the defining criteria of both phenomena are constantly shifting as culture changes. It is not a practice that just occurs in history; it is a matter that both signifies and reflects so much of what a culture owns and hides at any one moment.

The history of asylums and the history of mental illness are not the same thing. They intersect and are affected by each other, but there are different forces at work with the definition and management of both. Madness came to be seen as mental illness as a result of the medicalization of the asylums, as will be described in later pages. In short, what it refers to is a mindset that saw madness as a biologically driven illness, and therefore its treatment was increasingly placed into the hands of those who diagnosed the malady and prescribed somatic cures. This took the locus of the matter away from the interaction between society and individuals and focused it upon the biology of the mentally ill person; it obscured opportunity to develop any focus on the personality, history or trauma that may have been resident in the person diagnosed or the social environment which brought them to their diagnosis. It also shifted the responsibility for wellness away from the patient and their experiences and into the hands of the professional. This shift towards medicalization was part of the movement towards the professionalization of medicine which began with the establishment of the 1858 Medical Act and the establishment of the General Council of Medical Education and Registration. Medicalization of asylums was in part precipitated by a massive raft of abuses in the asylum system which provided the rationale for the shift, but it was not primarily spurred by the perceived benefits medicalization would have on the mentally ill. Rather it was a political move to place the asylums within the developing field of medicine, an attempt to register, manage and validate the treatment of the mentally ill within the discipline of the whole medical profession. There was a populist drive for all things to be done scientifically and there was a culture that dispersed the responsibility to the shoulders of scientists and doctors who were the clinical gatekeepers in what had become a potpourri of medical chicanery on the goldfields, and on the larger stage, right across the western colonial empires. This then, affected the understanding, the treatment and the status of those deemed mad, or mentally ill. (Gilman, 1987, 295)

Nineteenth century asylums evoke terrible images of dark and dirty cells, shrieking lunatics, horrible experiments, and abusive doctors. The disturbing nature of these impressions is not unfounded. Abuses and poor conditions in mental institutions have been well documented. Former patients often published sensational testimonies or witness statements revealing the dark and horrid nature of these secret places. Asylums have been associated with horror and secrecy because the reality of these institutions has been bleak and controversial ever since they became a part of the official structure of nineteenth and twentieth century western society. Isaac Hunt wrote of his experiences after three years incarceration in the lunatic asylum in Maine USA. He described the asylum as, 'a most iniquitous villainous system of inhumanity that would match the bloodiest days of the Inquisition or the tragedies of the Bastille'. (Hunt, 1851)

The asylum has been a favourite location of horror films and stories and yet the public cannot seem to get enough of them. Box Office successes 'One Flew over the Cuckoo's Nest', 'I never Promised you a Rose Garden' and 'The Cabinet of Dr Caligari' are widely acclaimed and viewed. But what is the attraction of such films? Why do they draw such interest and why is there such support for a thriving horror industry? Why are the asylums a popular haunt for ghost-tours and why has Aradale become known as 'the most haunted building in Australia'?

For most of its life Aradale was not primarily a place of healing but rather a place of degradation, torture and death. It is ironic that an institution created to house the insane in a benevolent, compassionate and curative manner, moving beyond the inhumanity of overcrowded, punitive madhouses and prisons, in time became a place of horror, terror and death for staff, patients and prisoners.

The word asylum means a place of shelter or refuge and a lunatic asylum was to be a place where those individuals suffering from mental torment could find refuge and safety. However, what we now know of the history of asylums, in terms of popular representations and various scandals and inquiries, is that patients were often mistreated and kept in dark and filthy cells. Asylums are often represented in popular culture as places where patients were experimented on and torture devices were commonly used as part of that experimentation. Furthermore, to be incarcerated in an asylum you did not have to commit any crime; it may have been a person gambled or drank too much or a husband wanted another woman or someone might have been sexually active with the wrong person, or the wrong sort of person. It might be that there was something different about an individual, the way they thought, acted, processed, responded. One did not need to have committed a crime to be placed in an asylum; much like refugees in an internment camp on Manus Island a detainee had no control over their destiny and might be forgotten about and die with no one ever knowing what happened or why. What could be more terrifying than that? A person committed to Aradale was the 'other', the person unlike those in society, and yet many of the people incarcerated in Aradale would not have seen themselves as any different to the rest of the populace. Anyone could end up a patient in Aradale. It became, in Jungian terms, the shadow of its culture, but even more, the shadow of what it was created to be, and every person carries, to some degree, some part of that shadow.

For Jung the shadow is 'the psyche's non-ego and yet an integral part of the objective psyche'. (Jung, 1954, para. 470) The shadow follows one around, as does a shadow, because it is a part of oneself; a failure to recognize, acknowledge and face the shadow aspects of ourselves is that which creates such incongruity. This is so not only at a personal level but also collectively; it infiltrates and infects groups, organizations and countries. It fuels prejudices between groups and ignites wars between nations.

Asylums as a Site of Horror

What is particularly pertinent here is the way in which asylums have become closely associated with horror, oppression and the dehumanization of marginalized people. In popular culture they are sites populated by people deemed horrific because of their supposed anti-human practices and thus a threat to the vulnerable public, but they are also sites of horror where the patients themselves become the victims of anti-human practices and monstrous designs by the institutions and staff. No one of these people on their own would have acted in the way described by the records of Aradale but the collective shadow has the power and force of many, not just one and as such is more potent, more frightening, more horror filled than the shadow of any one individual.

In popular imagination, asylums have come to represent the horrors associated with the anti-human; the asylum cannot be separated from the impact it has had on both the people associated with it nor can it be separated from the way society views mental illness. This complex weaving of people and space has serious implications for tourism at the defunct site of Aradale. Unlike gaols where the stigmatism is validated by the notion of misdeed, conviction and arrest, asylums are additionally problematic to the modern mind as more and more the tendency is to regard the patients or 'victims' as innocent. This fear of the patients via popular stigma against the mentally ill is exacerbated, perhaps bleakly ironically, by the fear of becoming one of the patients, caught up in the historic use of madness as a form of social control.

The social boundaries of the asylum are far more elusive than any physical divide they might feature, and the fictional expression of the asylum in popular media provides an orientation in society of the concerns, both historic and contemporary, surrounding such institutions. The boundaries of the asylum are thus fluid, with borders that act as a gradient rather than a cut-off. While the narrative of the asylum is hosted by physical locations such as Aradale it is also carried by those who have dwelt inside as patients or staff. The space of the asylum thus moves with them about society, carried with them in records and documentation, personal histories and a variety of other sources. And beyond those directly associated with the physical asylum itself, the narrative's fluid movement is affixed to those visible signs of deviance. And so, the haunting experience becomes more than simply a quirk of luck or a midnight thrill; it connects us to that traumatic and deeply problematic history and the social significance of the sites on which they occurred. As one of the Aradale ghost-tour guides reflected, 'Lunatic Asylums are the most haunted buildings because, unlike gaols whose inmates are convicted criminals, by today's standards many of these 'lunatics' were innocent, and we can relate more to madness than crime. And yet look at what these 'lunatics' endured. Incarceration, restraints, abuse and even sexual assault were part of their experience.'*

Popular Culture and the Asylum

In popular literature, news columns, websites and television specials, Aradale is regularly lauded as the most haunted site in Australia. It has even become the focus of several television programs and films such as *Haunting Australia*, *Mystical Guides Haunted Australia* and the forthcoming international horror film *Tujuh Bidadari*, all of which draw upon Aradale's reputation as a notorious haunted location, and so its reputation has grown in the public imagination. This is a pattern in common with many former Victorian era asylums around the world, and Aradale's representation is the site of some conflict between ghost-tour and dark tourism operators, and the descendants of former staff and patients who were incarcerated and treated within these walls. At base, it is a tension over differing representations of asylums as sites of terror and abuse or sites of curing and treatment, or as focal points for gothic popular culture.

This mixture of popular culture, history and folklore tends to provoke strong, if divided, responses to engagement with the past. These responses can, on the one hand, be characterized as dangerous, distasteful, inaccurate and exploitative, an example of what George referred to in her comment

* Personal communication with a guide from Eerie Tours 6.10.2019.

that 'popular culture is a wasteland of ignorance and hegemony, especially when it comes to the way the public abuses history.' (George, 2014, 9) Yet on the other hand these responses and their use of imaginative and evocative symbolic depictions of the traumas of the past can also be integral to the formation of community identity, emotional connection to the past, and reconciliation, all of which can become ideological statements of identity. There is also implied in this division a supposed difference between an empirical 'genuine historicity' and an imaginatively negotiated past shaped by folklore and popular culture, the notion that the public are passive receivers of mass messaging as opposed to being communities actively engaging, negotiating and creating meaning within their own shared cultural experience. In the case of the former Ararat asylum, this is complicated by the deeply ambivalent competing narratives upon which older archetypal mythic fears could be projected.

An underlying issue through all of these representations is the construction of the asylum in popular culture via literature and cinema. A key feature in this construction is the macabre overtones of the building itself, its imposing gothic imagery and the site atop 'Madman's Hill'. The very location of the former Ararat asylum, on a hill overlooking the town, its relative isolation, the imposing labyrinth of buildings with the enormous Victorian administration block dominating the skyline, all combine to create a uniquely ominous quality to the complex. The Ararat asylum came to inherit the literary legacy of other remote and magnificent structures in gothic and horror fiction as symbols of depression, torment and the unknown and here they create an uncanny liminal space for expectation and supernatural encounters. In gothic literature, the asylum acquired an uncanny dimension in which sensationalized portrayals of life within these institutions fused with ghosts of a traumatic past, monstrous and inhuman experiments and sadism on the part of both patients and attendants. In a sense the asylum, and the very real public concerns which emerged through public inquiries and newspaper coverage, became the receptacle in which older archetypal mythic fears could be projected.

H. P. Lovecraft used the asylum as the focal point of madness, the symbolic space encapsulating human realization of the indefinable horrors that lurk below the surface of a superficially mundane world. In contrast Stoker, in his most famous work 'Dracula', portrayed mental institutions as hopeless sites of neglect for incurable patients and the hapless victims of the vampire count. Other writers drew upon sensationalized depictions of horror and brutality to portray the asylum as a place of torment and fear. These narratives particularly drew on public fears surrounding the female lunatic, especially those with 'moral insanity' that threatened gendered norms and were configured as both a moral and physical threat to society which demanded incarceration. Further to this is the routine use of the asylum as an inherently threatening location in a plethora of video games such as Outlast, Thief, Arkham Asylum and Sanitarium. In cinema, the asylum has become a trope of popular horror and is almost always viewed as intrinsically unsettling. (Furse, 2014) As wiki tropes succinctly, if flippantly, comments,

> Poor Alice. She's lost her grip on sanity. She's stark raving mad. Surely what she needs to get well is a sleek modern psychiatric facility with freshly-washed sheets, nice nurses, and friendly doctors, just like the one Britney Spears keeps getting checked into.
>
> Yes, that's just what she needs. But what she'll get is Bedlam House, a dark, dank insane asylum straight out of the mid-18th to 19th century, staffed by Mad Doctors and Psycho Psychologists. Lobotomies in aisle four, sadistic Nurse Ratchet figures please report for surgery, slow descent from minor quirks in Cloudcuckoolanders to sitting in the corner mumbling cryptic phrases about Things Man Was Not Meant to Know and Eldritch Abominations will begin after your four o'clock slop from the creepy orderlies.
>
> Modern psychological techniques do not exist. Electroshock therapy is handed out like lollipops at the

> doctor's office – and we're not talking modern, painless electroshock, we're talking high voltage screaming shocks. Those padded walls haven't been scrubbed in weeks and even if they had been, the inmates would just keep writing on them. And sure, there may be straitjackets in the wardrobe, but patients are just as likely to be chained to the wall. Abandon all hope, ye who enter Bedlam House!
>
> (https://tvtropes.org/pmwiki/pmwiki.php/Main/BedlamHouse)

These fictional and artistic representations exist in a mutually formative relationship with mass media coverage, drawing on sensationalist reportage whilst at the same time constructing the popular notions of the asylum in which these reports were written and interpreted. The resultant matrix of representations is inherently cyclical; the fictional representation generates interest in dark tourism at asylums while the history of the sites continues to inform popular culture. This process fundamentally underlies the use of ghostly, horrific stories of incarceration and abuse by popular culture as vehicles for memorializing trauma at these sites, as is clearly apparent at Aradale, a contemporary dark tourism site in which the crumbling buildings become a focal point of horror through stories of abuse and neglect and through fear of the lunatics themselves as potential perpetrators of anti-human practices.

As Jenkins argues, one of the most consistent culturally coded images in contemporary western popular culture is the notion of the haunted asylum. (Jenkins, 2003, 3) It is manifested in the representation of the ominous institution characterised by walls and gothic architecture within which is bounded a dark world of bleak institutional corridors, padded cells, threat and trauma posed by fear of both insanity and the insane. In this sense, asylums are places of loss, places where memory, sanity, identity and status face dissolution in the face of the madness making machine of the institution and where feelings of grief and loss are common triggers for mental and physical breakdown. (Luckins, 2003, 170) Within these walls the ghosts of patients living in abandonment and isolation occupy the imagination in stories of tragedy, lost loves and rave in anger and torment under the weight of institutional power, ostracization and madness. As Walter writes,

> Lost to themselves, stripped of their personal agency and humanity, ghostly patients endure not only spiritual and mental anguish but also relive the physical pain they once experienced at the hands of medical professionals. The spirits of these nurses and physicians are often reportedly trapped within the asylum's walls. While the ghosts of nurses sometimes serve as motherly figures who protect their wards against pain and suffering, they are more often subservient to wicked physicians who subject defenceless and voiceless patients to torturous therapies such as electroshock, sensory deprivation, ice-water baths, and lobotomies. The spectral physicians who stalk the haunted hospital are often rumoured to have performed illegal experiments such as vivisection on their patients in order to fulfil their sadistic sexual desires or to advance medical research and inflate their professional reputation. The perversion and rapacity of these physicians is believed to have been so powerful in life that their spirits not only continue to torment the invisible inmates of the asylum but also pose a physical threat to curious members of the living who might venture in to investigate. (Walter, 2014, 51–2)

Whilst narratives surrounding the building and construction of mental hospitals in government documents and public pronouncements are presented as panaceas for the abuses of the past, overwhelmingly, through popular culture, scandal and folklore these asylums are depicted as places of terror in which the most vulnerable are subjected to the all-pervasive power of malevolent madmen, sadistic staff and the 'mad doctors' who wielded absolute power in this liminal space outside of the public gaze in these forgotten spaces.

Superficially, the association of horror and terror with asylums and hospitals seems a strange association to make. Asylums and hospices refer to places of refuge and care. Sanitas refers to health and wellbeing. Certainly, in the etymological development of the terms and the laudable goals presented by the initial advocates of these places, the space of the asylum should be associated with care and rehabilitation. But as Walter argues, the modern vision of the mental hospital and asylum represent deeply entrenched archetypes surrounding our own culturally constructed and deeply conflicted beliefs about the nature of those we deem mad and the fear and guilt surrounding those we have ostracized from our social world through the process of labelling, and our own fear of exclusion. These archetypally reflect our projected shadows and anxiety surrounding our own tenuous grip on sanity, our own fear of exclusion and vulnerability. Yet perhaps ironically, these representations in folklore and popular culture, while drawing attention to abuses and traumas of the past, often kept removed from the public gaze, also work to objectify the patients of these institutions and caricaturize the complex histories within them involving relationships between patients and staff.

Aradale in Dark Tourism

The Aradale complex was finally closed in 1998 as part of a general state-wide policy of deinstitutionalization, however there had already been a slow drawn out process of closure and shifting patients to community care since the early 1990s. Another important issue regarding the significance of the lunatic asylum as a heritage site is its overwhelming importance to the economy and society of Ararat and the surrounding region. For one hundred and thirty years the asylum was the primary source of employment and generated enormous income for the town. Employing thousands of people from the region over the course of its history, the asylum's social and economic significance to the district defies overstatement. The implications for the community of so many people being closely involved in the industry of incarceration and mental illness are enormous. Inasmuch as the site represents a manifestation of the history of psychology and treatment of mental illness, it also represents a history of the town of Ararat. Since 2015 the grounds have been utilized by NMIT (Northern Melbourne Institute of TAFE) as a campus facility for the Australian College of Wine while the original building complex has become a heritage tourism site for the 'Friends of J Ward' who organize daytime heritage tours, and the 'Eerie Tours' franchise who guide tourists and paranormal investigators on ghost, dark history and supernatural investigation tours in the late evenings.

One of the most vivid representations of the competing narratives concerning Aradale is the extent to which these are extraordinarily polarized in the contradictory descriptions framed by the Friends of J Ward and Eerie Tours. In the first case, the site is represented as a locus of community while, conversely, the night tours transform the institution into a place of horror and trauma. The Friends of J Ward tours during the day feature anecdotes of patient life, friendly stories of staff and patient cricket matches and a few risqué episodes, such as a nurse being caught smuggling her boyfriend through a laundry chute. Some mention is made of more infamous patients such as the self-mutilating Garry David but by and large the focus of the story is on the asylum as a site of community. These tours cater predominantly to the friends and family of former staff and patients with negative experiences being cast as peripheral aberrations from the norm. Indeed, deinstitutionalization and the closing of the asylum is represented as a community tragedy with a Friends of J Ward spokesman commenting that,

> People are still quite bitter about the closing of the place. I think it had to be. A lot of people felt this place was doing a great job and it had a place in Ararat society and in the society of Victoria for that matter. Aradale was a major employer in Ararat for decades and holds a special place in the community. (https://www.abc.net.au/news/2017-10-21/looking-back-in-time-at-ararats-mental-asylum/9072024)

At night however, the buildings are transformed into a site of gothic horror in which guests are taken on lantern-guided tours that feature stories of horrific abuse, ghostly visitations and neglect. Crucial to this reconfiguration is the notion of Aradale being a 'haunted' site with a vast array of multi-media representations of the asylum complex as 'Australia's Most Haunted Building'. These contrasting depictions of Aradale are the source of considerable friction in the Ararat community as the descendants of former staff and patients compete with the ghost-tour industry in shaping the narratives associated with Aradale as a heritage site.

These polarized representations of the Ararat Lunatic Asylum have been closely reflected in media coverage of the location since its inception. In particular, print media over the past one hundred and thirty years has tended to alternate between glowing depictions of the institution as a place of caring and healing for the disadvantaged and damaged, and exposures of instances of abject horror, murder and sexual abuse. The initial articles about the Ararat Lunatic Asylum in the *Argus*, for example, feature glowing commendation for the building's sophistication of design, self-sufficiency and ingeniousness that would surely create an ideal environment to care for the mentally ill and avoid the chaos of Bedlam (Bethlem Mental Hospital in London). (*Argus*, 14.12.1866, 6) One also gets a sense of immense pride in the community regarding the enormity of the project. Similar articles praising reform, the care of the doctors and accounts of the benefits to patients, are also commonly found in newspaper reports. However, other stories recounted in the print media illustrated quite a different image of the location, featuring staggering examples of patient mistreatment, sexual assault and neglect. In particular, the 1883 case of Matilda Cutler who was released into her husband's custody after considerable time at the Ararat Lunatic Asylum was reported in detail in Australian newspapers. Her story, as reported in the *Argus*, *Ararat Advertiser* and other newspapers, revealed shocking examples of abuse including regular beatings and lacerations, involuntary confinement, use of freezing water and restraints as punishment, and the horrific tale of a woman who died as the result of an attendant ramming a metal spoon down her throat. Similarly, late nineteenth century newspaper reportage of the asylum also routinely featured examples of patients who engaged in murders, violence and sexual assault. In one example a woman, evidently suffering from post-natal depression, became so filled with anxiety over her inability to prevent her child crying that she slit its throat and as a result spent the rest of her life in the asylum. (*Bendigo Advertiser*, 17.8.1894, 3) More recent reports have also been divided between representations of the site as a place of healing and a place of horror. The *Herald Sun* in 2014 for example, publicized a multi-page article on the asylum entitled 'Victorian psychiatric patients' grim fate in hellish 1800s hospitals', with a litany of horrors brought forward from asylum records. (https://www.heraldsun.com.au/news/victoria/victorian-psychiatric-patients-grim-fate-in-hellish-1800s-hospitals/news-story/c7928ebe8a9f527a941cce86e0990fef) Overall, public reporting on inquiries has tended to be divided between sensationalist stories about 'horror hospitals' and those which advocate the site as a maligned place of healing and care.

A Contested History

Of import into the site's closure as a mental hospital, the widely publicized 1991 investigative task force into cases of abuse within the asylum read as a litany of horrors. While the overall findings were of systemic neglect and corruption, 20–50% of food not finding its way to patients, wide-spread theft, patient confinement and a culture of dependency, the team did not find evidence of systemic sexual and physical abuse in relation to specific allegations but concluded that the culture of dependency and boredom created an environment in which such events could occur with relative impunity. Nevertheless, the scale of specific allegations made by former staff and patients were of such horror as to beggar belief and the corresponding response by management and local police could not help but create the impression of deliberate ignorance of such occurrences. In one example, an accusation that female patients were being pressed into prostitution for a small group of volunteers in exchange for cigarettes, with a vivid depiction of a violent sexual assault, was met with the claim by police that 'the issue of consent was confused, given the women were allegedly asking for cigarettes as payment for intercourse'. (VPARL, 1988–92, no. 198) One ponders that, irrespective of the truth of the claim surrounding the exchange of cigarettes, such behavior speaks of a horrendous culture of boredom, neglect, violence and systemic dependency. A review of staff disciplinary actions (VPRS 18303) does discuss a comparatively small number of allegations featuring assaults, sexual assaults and neglect, all of which are disciplined according to policy, yet as research on the Kew Asylum by Monk has shown, when compared to records of patient injuries and other documentation there is undoubtedly a high degree of under reporting of such incidents in the Ararat asylum's history. (Monk, 2007) An evaluation of the seclusion register reveals some disturbing indicators, such as a woman placed into seclusion for the maximum time per day of eight hours for over four months under the heading 'spirited'. (VPRS 18137) These stories, the folklore they represent and the rather limp responses by management and local police to such extraordinary allegations undoubtedly contributed to Aradale's negative reputation in the broader community and media representation and deservedly so. Yet articles discussing aspects of darker history can often be met by polarized public responses, on one side from former staff and their descendants defending the institution, and on the other those decrying claims of horrid conditions and treatment of patients. The following comment is illustrative of public responses in defense of Aradale's legacy.

> My question is, do the people who are running the Aradale Ghost Tours and posting this comparison actually have any personal experience of working in the institution before its closure? While Aradale in its early years may have been like many other similar institutions at the time, as times and trends in care changed, so did the way those in Aradale were cared for. Many people who follow this page have family members and friends who worked at Aradale or indeed

worked there themselves and find the comparison appalling! I'm not saying every staff member was perfect however the overwhelming majority were hard workers who genuinely cared for those they were caring for. Don't believe every rumour you may have heard about conditions in Aradale. It's an insult to those who worked there and genuinely cared 😠. (https://www.facebook.com/AradaleGhostTours/)

These divisions in representation persist to the present day and there are deep scars in the community wrought not only by the asylum and its legacy but also by the economic damage inflicted when such a large employer closed its doors with devastating impact on the town's economy. In George's research into Pennhurst she argues that disability activists attempted to achieve a 'sanctification' of the heritage site by redefining the story of the closure as a symbol of progress in the rights of the mentally ill through community-based activism. This is also the case with Aradale and popular representations of deinstitutionalization at the site, despite protests from the Friends of J Ward to the contrary. Paradoxically, this version of the narrative requires a representation of the site as a symbol of repression, abuse and neglect of patients and draws upon caricatures of the asylum reminiscent of gothic horror, thus providing fertile fodder for the current use of the site as a haunted attraction. In contrast, Friends of J Ward focused their narrative on memories that represented Aradale as a symbol of the community, public service and genuine care for patients. To this clique, these darker narratives were inherently threatening as they compromised local community views of the town's history and the memories associated with the thousands of townsfolk, relatives and friends who were employed at the Asylum in its 130-year history. There are similar concerns raised by families who had relatives incarcerated there and felt the need to defend their actions. Like Pennhurst, the public representation of the site was controversial and divided because the closure of the institution itself was controversial. It represented a profound attack on the local economy as well as fundamentally compromising people's familial and personal sense of values and identity. (Kelly, 2014, iv) Indeed, a review of letters to the editor in the local papers and social media indicated that many members of the local public believed the institution should not have been closed and were personally threatened by efforts to sanctify closure as an example of progress and by the recasting of Aradale as the locus of an attraction rooted in gothic horror.

Zerubavel referred to these kinds of public conversations as mnemonic battles in which communities engage in conflict over representations of the past, how their stories should be memorialized and who has control over the representations. (Zerubavel, 1996, 283) The representation of Aradale has been shaped by these conflicts between former patients, staff and the ghost tour industry. This mnemonic battle of representations has been waged through mass media coverage shaped by the intersection of popular culture, history and folklore. In particular, the tension revolves around the intersecting issues of positive and negative representations of the site and its heritage as well as concerns that the publicization of traumatic experiences by patients has been commercialized and colored by the ghost tour industry and reduced to a tormented image shaped by popular notions of asylums in gothic horror. As George argues in her dissertation on the commodification of the Pennhurst Asylum via dark tourism, 'the stories of journalists and advocates, which were intended to expose real suffering and injustice, unintentionally paved the way for the attraction's parody of Pennhurst.' (George, 2014, 205) This has been further complicated by advocates for patients who experienced abuse in the asylum and found their narratives entwined and appropriated for use in tourism. (Kelly, 2014, 2005) The ghost hunting programs, horror films and dark history/ghost tour models applied to the Ararat Asylum follow patterns common to other representations of historic sites in popular culture. Foote argues that this pattern of appropriation may lead to the process of 'obliteration', as the artefacts of history become reconstituted as examples of folklore and popular culture, (Foote, 2003, 25) following in the footsteps of Jameson's hypothesis that in the era of late capitalism, genuine historicity becomes supplanted by commodified images within the broader framework of consumable culture. (Jameson, 1991, 19) The former Ararat asylum has now been utilized as a site of haunting by numerous television programs and films such as *Haunting Australia* (https://www.imdb.com/title/tt3526418/), *Mystical Guides Haunted Australia* (https://www.imdb.com/title/tt4928516/locations) and the international horror film *Tujuh Bidadari* (https://www.imdb.com/title/tt9160672/). These films, drawing on the unique visual qualities of the site and its history, have been deeply enmeshed in broader representations of the asylum and mental illness from gothic literature and popular culture. They also draw on a broader folkloric mythology of spirits as a romanticized memorialization of trauma. The narratives associated with the site have thus become a complex, mutually formative web of history, traumatic experiences, commodification and popular culture serving the interests of diverse sectors of the community making claim over the site and its heritage.

This mixture of popular culture, history and folklore provoke strong, if divided, responses to engagement with the past and these responses can, in one sense, be characterized as dangerous, distasteful, inaccurate and exploitative, an example of what George referred to in her comment that 'popular culture is a wasteland of ignorance and hegemony, especially when it comes to the way the public abuses history.' (George, 2014, 9) Yet on the other hand these representations and their use of imaginative and evocative symbolic depictions of the traumas of the past can also be integral to the formation of community identity, emotional connection to the past and reconciliation, all of which can become ideological statements of identity. (Waldron, 2008, 228) There is also, implied in this division between an empirical 'genuine historicity' and an imaginatively negotiated past shaped by folklore and popular culture, the notion that the public are passive receivers of mass messaging, as opposed to being communities actively engaging, negotiating and creating meaning within their own shared cultural experience. (Hariman and Lucaites, 2008, 35; Hooper-Greenhill, 2007, 76) In the case of Aradale, this is complicated by the already deeply ambivalent competing narratives in popular culture surrounding insane asylums as sites of both healing and incarceration, where patients are represented both as passive victims and dangerous predators. The ghost-tour industry, interestingly, only focusses on the latter, on the horror, the dysfunction, the incarceration and the predation. Partly, this is because the public would not come to a ghost tour that focussed on the nice and the comforting. They come because the ghost genre facilitates an experience of the horror.

In the psyche of the individual and/or community, the phenomenon of ghosts and specters is a kind of 'entanglement' between history and the unconscious which is given expression through experiences connected to unsettlement, displacement, transgression, repressed anxiety and loss of security. On behalf of the community, ghosts and paranormal activity enact the fear, the displacement, the dislocation and the unspoken. (Jung, 1981, 367) As the ghost researcher John Sabol argues, 'What emerges (or materializes) is a re-assemblage of what still remains, the "ghost". The use of a creative experiential, entangled, and relational archaeology in the present can engage in those spaces in which the past intervenes today in the present "haunted sites"'. (Sabol, 2015, 13) In this context ghosts and hauntings are a window into the internal workings of both individual and society. As such, the window requires an exploration of what it reveals, and hides, and what we are to comprehend of the dynamics that are at work in the 'weltanschauung' of Aradale.

2

The Birth of the Australian Asylum

Madness in the Colonies

> Confined on a ship, from which there is no escape, the madman is delivered to the river with its thousand arms, the sea with its thousand roads, to that great uncertainty external to everything. He is a prisoner in the midst of what is freest, the openest of routes: bound fast at the infinite crossroads … And the land he will come to is unknown – as is, once he disembarks, the land from which he comes. (Foucault, 1967, 11)

The early nineteenth century saw a vast expansion of purpose-built asylums across the western world and particularly through the British Empire. Not even its farthest outposts in South Africa, India, Asia and Australia escaped the rapid growth of purpose-built asylums. In Britain itself, David Wright estimates over three hundred thousand people were confined in newly built asylums in Britain and Wales while in Australia the population confined to asylums came to exceed one in three hundred people. (Wright, 1997)

The patterns of confinement were indiscriminate, transcending class, ethnic and gendered divides, yet also creating new patterns in the public perception of confinement and mental illness, reflecting their own networks of prejudice and structural disadvantage. As Wright argues, while Foucault was incorrect in his understanding of the chronology of the period of the 'Great Confinement', he nonetheless accurately reflected the transformative impact of the global asylum system on the social, cultural and political landscape of the British Empire and its colonies. (Wright, 1997)

Throughout the early nineteenth century a growing lunacy reform movement transformed the understanding of mental illness from a miscellaneous network of beliefs rooted in religious superstition and perceptions of criminality and sin, to the enlightenment view that madness could be treated and cured as a disease if given proper treatment within an institution. Prior to this, care for the mentally ill was relegated to an ad hoc system of treatment governed by the poor laws but enacted within local communities through social ostracism, the care of charitable bodies and commonly, through the criminal system. The 'Poor Act' of 1601 established committees based in each administrative parish, consisting of representatives of local wealthy and powerful families and the church; these were to levy finances for the case of the 'lame, impotent, old, blind and such other among them, being poor and not able to work'. (Bartlet, 1993) The mentally ill who could not be easily integrated into the community or who were not imprisoned for perceived criminal or blasphemous activities, by and large fell into this broad association of the deserving and undeserving poor, depending on social circumstances. In the era of the industrial revolution these measures increasingly came to be manifested in the institution of the workhouse. By the time of Australia's first colonization there were over one hundred and twenty workhouses in England alone suffering from overcrowding, squalid conditions and high mortality rates. The inmates of these institutions were a mix of criminals who had escaped the hulks on the Thames, widows, alcoholics, abandoned wives and women who had become pregnant out of wedlock, those who disturbed the public peace and the long term unemployed. In short, the 'undeserving poor' who had the misfortune to fall on the margins of society and social respectability. (Bonwick, 1996, 11)

The diagnosis of madness or mental illness was seen as cause for legitimate professional control, the latest phase in the enactment of disciplinary power in western society that had been going on since the eighteenth century. (Foucault, 1967, 162) The process of labelling and incarcerating the mad had some analogies with the sixteenth century witch trials; these were also premised on scapegoating and undiscerning labelling of those deemed outside the norm, as 'other', that is 'not me' (Miller, 1961, 34). Scapegoating means finding those who can be identified with the evil occurring in a community, blamed for it and cast out of the community in order to leave the remaining members with a feeling of absolution and safety. By demonizing others, scapegoating enables a society to maintain the illusion of its own innocence and so occlude responsibility for the social dysfunction or suffering in which they are embroiled. According to analytical psychology, scapegoating reveals more about the perpetrators of judgement than it does of those deemed to be the culprits; it reveals that which has been concealed, the shadow. A scapegoating community carries the shadow, that which is put out of sight, not seen and yet is – and must be suppressed. But the suppression of the shadow is very costly and demands great resources and energy and is, eventually, very damaging not only to the victims but to the whole community.

The process of defining a person as mad or mentally ill, can easily be a form of scapegoating. The community determines what is normal, what defines the boundaries of desired behaviour, thoughts and feelings and brings to bear all its combined force to sustain that platform and assert that it is good. Any person who finds such an arrangement 'maddening', must be defined as mad so that the community can assert its own virtue. The fear of the stigma associated with madness thus serves to ensure self-policing, self-surveillance and self-mentoring of behaviour, to avoid being labelled as mad.

It is argued that the practice of enforcing regulation of what is sane upon the society, undertaken by the church in the witch trials era for example, has simply in the modern era been passed on to the experts in the field of psychiatry who monitor and regulate psychosocial well-being and individual functioning. In this context, madness may be understood as the experience of unresolved difficulties in functioning within a society and the term madness could be apportioned to any protest of the powerless that causes disruption to the comfort of a given controlling social group (Goffman, 1990, 4–5) As the sociologist Andrew Scull argues, the designation 'madness' is a useful tool 'to get rid of troublesome people for the rest of us ...' (Scull, 1978, 260) The incarceration of Dr Carr, a clinician of the Yarra Bend and Aradale institutions may be a poignant example. An outspoken critic of the squalor and brutality the patients of these institutions suffered, Carr also ran afoul of the Yarra Bend Asylum superintendent and following a heated argument with his wife, Carr was thereafter designated mad by the Superintendent, incarcerated in Yarra Bend, then Aradale, and never released. He died a 'mad' person according to those powerful people whom he had criticised and offended. The question remains as to where the madness really lay, in the deplorable conditions that Dr Carr criticised, or in the man deemed mad.

The key principle of these institutions was that maladjustment and mental illness were the product of sin which came from idleness, promiscuity and uselessness, the only cure for which was hard work enforced with discipline. Infamously this culture of hard labour and austere conditions enforced upon people who were believed to have earned their fate through sinfulness, often degenerated into simple brutality. Solitary confinement, beatings, enforced starvation, enduring the freezing cold and baking heat along with brutal back-breaking labour were commonplace and validated as a mechanism for purging the unfortunates of their uselessness and idleness through suffering. As one workhouse boasted 'If wild beasts can be broken at the yoke, it must not be despaired of when correcting the strayed.' (Foucault, 1967, 63) Medical care in asylums was extremely haphazard and erratic with irregular annuities for payment of medical treatment yet also driven by an ideology which saw mental illness as a sign of human weakness to be expunged by labour and strict discipline. Very commonly those who had acted in a criminal way and were deemed insane, those suffering from mental illness, and people who simply suffered the misfortune of unemployment or abandonment and were unable to cope in the chaotic transformation of industrialization were integrated together in these institutions.

People suffering from mental illness, along with many others, struggled to comply with Britain's increasingly strict and complicated vagrancy laws which were designed to manage the vast displacement wrought by industry. This was exacerbated by the conflicts between the need for a mobile population to accommodate rapid urbanization and the loss of ancestral farmland and the commons with legacy laws designed to restrict migration under feudalism. In one instance it was illegal to leave one's place of settlement, typically the village one was born in, without due means of support yet at the same time it was no longer possible to reside in these villages given the loss of the commons and rapid transformation of agricultural production. Given the ongoing frustrations and inevitable sense of loss and anger at this rapid period of transformation it is unsurprising that many thousands, indeed hundreds of thousands of people fell afoul of this 'great confinement', especially those suffering from mental illness. Although some legislative policies were enacted to restrict the mixing of the mentally ill with violent criminals, such as the report on the Select Committee for the Insane in 1763, in practice the policies were ignored especially given the primitive understanding of insanity during the eighteenth century. (Jones, 1972, 198–212)

Another difficulty in understanding the fate and numbers of those afflicted with mental illness in the eighteenth and early nineteenth centuries were the significant number of people who, despite apparent mental illness were not recorded and were kept secret by their families through fear of public shame and embarrassment. Kept confined by their families, sometimes for a lifetime, these people existed in the shadows of folklore and popular fiction, stories of lunatics kept in the attic and under the stairs such as exemplified by the mysterious and tragic figure Bertha Antionette Mason of Jane Eyre described thusly,

> In the deep shade, at the farther end of the room, a figure ran backwards and forwards. What it was, whether beast or human being, one could not, at first sight, tell... it snatched and growled like some strange wild animal: but it was covered with clothing, and a quantity of dark, grizzled hair, wild as a mane, hid its head and face. (Bronte, 2000)

Underlying the growing rates of insanity was the problem of what madness meant to people in the eighteenth and early nineteenth centuries. The law of the day clearly defined the people who were authorised to make the decision that a person's behaviour was bizarre enough to warrant incarceration in a lunatic asylum, but the interpretation and enactment of that warrant was profoundly open to personal influence. The Crown's jurisdiction over the estates and persons of lunatics and idiots had been codified in British law since the late middle ages, and the confinement of the insane was never just a medical or social matter; it also involved the law and so related to issues of power and social control.

The 'Mad Doctors'

The mad doctors, the doctors who had oversight of the asylums, were subject to legal regulations which defined standards of practice, incarceration and treatment. But these were also shaped by political pressures of social expectation, personal relationships, gender roles and class. In this context, what was defined as madness in the Georgian era was as much about social construct as it was about defining a pathology that might be clinically described as mental illness in today's context. The symptoms and diagnosis of madness were manufactured as a by-product of cultural values, and because these values vary greatly according to place, time and circumstance, the definition of madness was, and is infinitely fluid; it is a comparative reality in that an individual who transgresses what is acceptable might be labelled as mad compared to those who stay within the boundaries of what is considered normal. But this will vary according to time, place and culture, especially in a time of such tumult as the industrial revolution.

From this perspective, madness and sanity are not easily definable. 'Normality' is prescribed by the predominant social order in a society and is embedded in the moral and traditional values by which that society imagines it attains cohesion. Any society has a vested interest in stigmatising those they define as mad, those who deviate from what is accepted as permissible by the rest of the community, because by doing so they are discouraging that which is a threat to social order, and they are defining that threat as being outside of social order. Michel Foucault argues,

> The analyses of our psychologists and sociologists, which turn the patient into a deviant and which seek the origin of the morbid in the abnormal, are therefore above all a projection of cultural themes. In fact, a society expresses itself positively in the mental illnesses manifested by its members;
>
> ... whether it places them at the centre of its religious life, as is often the case among primitive people; or whether it seeks to expatriate them outside social life, as does our own culture. (Foucault, 1967, 104–5)

Michel Foucault famously represented asylums as vehicles of social control and defined their use as essentially, 'madness making machines'. (Foucault, 1967, 69) The asylum's function often resulted in an institution designed to shape categories of people labelled as 'mad' within a mutually formative social discourse of knowledge and power around a social construction of madness. As Elizabeth Willis argues in relation to Australia's asylums:

> Each asylum straddled the illusory boundary between an institution with an obvious punitive character and one with an ostensibly non-punitive character. As a hospital, it professed to be able to cure the sick; as a place for those

> whose behaviour was not acceptable outside, it was a place of incarceration, of confinement. (Willis, 1999)

Throughout history, madness has been used as a means of separating out from society that which is unacceptable and underlining the idea of what is normal within a given political and social construct. For this reason, what is seen to be madness is commonly experienced both by individuals and by the community as threatening its cohesion. This felt threat reflects, perpetuates and reinforces the acceptable and the not acceptable and thereby perpetuates and protects the status quo. In the time of our focus, a white woman falling in love with a black man would have been designated as mad. In our current culture, discrimination against such a coupling would be designated as criminal.

The commonly used term 'madness' cannot be understood therefore in isolation from the prevailing understandings of madness and sanity and the expressions of those applications in law and popular culture. In the era within our exploration, madness was perceived as a signifier of deviance. Because mental health was seen to be that stance of mind and behaviour which is socially acceptable, madness was seen as a wilful deviation from that, thus requiring sanction and coercion to motivate or enable the perpetrator to conform to social expectations. For this reason, madness and lunacy encapsulated a very broad net over much of society and included many categories that today would be defined within other terminology such as poverty, protest and trauma.

Prior to the eighteenth century, the control of deviance from the norm had been a communal and familial responsibility. The poor and powerless, the rather nebulous class of the morally disreputable, those people who had a physical or mental disability, petty criminals, vagrants and the insane were managed by similar mechanisms. Characteristically, little effort was made to segregate these from others. Lunatics were generally treated no differently from deviants; a few of the more violent or troublesome may have found themselves incarcerated in ad hoc confinement, or if this was impracticable, relegated to the rather diverse prison population. (Fessler, 1956, 901) According to Andrew Scull,

> Those who had lost their wits formed part of the much larger group of the poor, the morally disreputable, the crippled, the orphaned, the aged and the maimed. (Scull, 1978, 125)

A prime example of this fusion between the medieval poor laws and the burgeoning initialization of the prison and medical systems was the monastic hospital of Bethlem which became synonymous with madness and the abuse of the mentally ill in the eighteenth and early nineteenth centuries. Whilst from the late sixteenth century there were a number of hospitals which specialised in care of the mentally ill, most notably in York, the longevity of Bethlem and its dark reputation gave it a unique role in the popular perception of mental illness and the notoriety given to asylums in popular culture. It is from Bethlem Hospital that 'Bedlam' entered the English language as a euphemism for chaos and madness.

Established in the thirteenth century as a priory, it was turned into a hospice for the care of the insane in the fourteenth century and in the sixteenth century came under the auspices of the city of London where it remained until the post war era. In 1674 it was destroyed in a fire and rebuilt in the model of classical architecture in imitation of the French Royal Palace and became a significant tourist attraction for the City of London. Partly this was due to the beautiful ornamentation of its façade, but predominantly for the spectacle of the insane. Visitors to the hospital could watch the antics of the insane as well as floggings and draconian treatments such as bleedings, emetics and hot/cold 'baths' for the price of a penny. As Bonwick discusses, it was a wealthy institution, well supported by donations, tourism and investments, yet patients, although supported by relatives and parish subscriptions, often resided in appalling conditions. Those who were discharged from Bedlam, known colloquially as Toms O'Bedlam, were giving an identifying badge and permission to beg without fear of the vagrancy or poor laws. (Bonwick, 1996, 14) Clearly this situation was inappropriate for the care of the insane and sat at odds with the rising medicalization of how mental illness was perceived. Pressure grew on parliament for a more systematic and rational approach to the governing of madness in the British Empire.

The First Asylums

The first act for the treatment of the insane in its modern institutional context was in 1714, and it began the slow process towards recognition of insanity as a medical condition and the eventual development of 'private madhouses' under registered management and care of lay and medical people. While initially these were few and only open to the wealthiest of patron families, by the early nineteenth century there were close to a hundred and fifty operating in Britain. The most opulent of these provided accommodation, care, treatment and recreational activities for the economic elite and nobility of eighteenth century Britain. For the majority, these madhouses often became places of infamous neglect and cruelty. One example, cited by Bonwick, described an area of one such asylum;

> The accommodation consisted of 6 cells 9 feet by 5 feet opening onto a passage which in turn look onto a pigsty and dung heap. The walls were damp greenstone; there was no light or ventilation except when the cell door was open. The patients were chained to their beds. Of the 14 patients only one was not confined in irons. (Bonwick, 1996, 10)

Some institutions in the late eighteenth century did experiment with a less draconian approach to mental illness and in the cases where it was recognized that those suffering from mental illness were unable to work it removed the stain of sinfulness and immorality, replacing these with the term 'unfortunate'. Some locations began to separate the insane from the general population, such as the Mint Workhouse in Bristol which established wards for the care of the insane and employed medical personnel for that care. As time progressed this led to the Mint Workhouse eventually transforming into the Bristol Lunatic Asylum. (Bonwick, 1996, 14) A key instigation of this push for reform was the 'Moral Treatment' of the insane, a concept pioneered by Phillipe Pinel (1745–1826). The foundation of Moral Treatment was gaining the patient's confidence by kind treatment and solicitude for their welfare. (Pinel, 1806, 9) This called for a new approach to the care of the mentally ill, perceiving them not as sinners who needed to be punished for their moral transgressions but rather, like errant children, people who could be cured through 'the vigilance of a kind and affectionate parent who never lost sight of the principles of a most genuine philanthropy'. (Shipley, 1961, 294) The Moral Treatment approach argued that the most helpful way to treat mental illness was through the forming of a warm, therapeutic environment where patients had personalised care, access to medical treatment, and were encouraged in manual labour which would in turn offer some remuneration to the patient. Asylums were to be clean and comfortable with attractive and pleasant views, comfortable gardens and caring attendants. This stood in stark contrast to the workhouses embedded in older approaches to mental health founded on penal servitude and redolent with abuse and the religious notion of purifying the soul through suffering. Even though Moral Treatment's noble ideal was seldom realised in practice, it became an increasingly important ideal to aspire to. Likewise, it became the source of many scandals in its unrealised ideals, specifically in the shape of inquiries into the asylum system which came to dominate care for the mentally ill.

In the early stages of the lunacy reform movement the care of the mentally ill was increasingly absorbed into 'hybrid' institutions which, under the poor laws, accepted paupers, charitable, and private patients. (Smith, 1995) Typically, these institutions were organized under a lay system of governors in conjunction with local poor law authorities. The ad hoc nature of this approach tended to lead to a wide variety of approaches within the context of local social, cultural and economic concerns, personal beliefs and politics. This was particularly pertinent regarding the role of medical practitioners as they began to integrate within the burgeoning asylum system and had significant consequences regarding the access and type of treatment that could be afforded to patients. Given the poor level of understanding of the human mind, treatment in the late eighteenth through nineteenth centuries was extremely rudimentary and in some cases could seem quite bizarre to a modern perspective. For example, Schroeder Van Der Kolk, whose work was translated in Melbourne during the 1860s, lists a wide variety of pseudoscientific and bizarre treatments applied to patients, including freezing baths and showers, cupping, bleeding, electro galvanic shocks, scarification, isolation, and leeches applied to the anus (as a cure for masturbation). (Van der Kolk, 1870) As we will see later in this chapter, a common complaint was that the barbaric treatments in practice served more often as a punishment for difficult patients than as genuine therapeutic treatments. Likewise, medication was limited to a variety of tinctures, tartar emetics, camphor and large quantities of opioids. Much of this was driven by a perception of the human mind viewed through the lens of renaissance thought regarding humours and religious manias. (Dax, 1981, 257) One example, as cited in a manual translated for use in Australian asylums was described thus,

> On admission she was quite confused and had various insane ideas, which after a few days passed into quiet mania. The eyes had a dull expression, and the woman generally lay obtuse, and half unconscious. She used to press her hand against her forehead, which action, doubtless, had its origin in the still present severe headache, but of which she, in her half or completely unconscious or comatose state, only slightly complained. But of a local lesion of the brain, there could then be no doubt. Derivative measures, an antiphlogistic treatment with leeches, and later some doses of camphor, were of very little use. (Van der Kolk, 1870, 71)

Contrasting markedly from these sort of treatments, the 'Moral Treatment' model of mental health care was initially closely associated with religious institutions such as the York Retreat and was heavily supported in Quakerism. In the wake of King George's madness becoming known to the public, Moral Treatment gained in popularity as public concern and outrage escalated over the treatment of mental illness. Increasing scandals associated with Bethlem Mental Hospital occupied considerable space in the print media of the early nineteenth century. The Moral Treatment model offered a paternalistic approach to mental health which was readily co-opted by the medical fraternity eager to distance themselves from the religious superstitions of the past, and offered a salve to the conscience of those whose loved ones were incarcerated within asylum institutions. This led to a push for asylums to be increasingly under the control of medical personnel rather than the entrenched networks of wealthy families and the church which had dominated the older system under the poor laws. New legislation was hurried through parliament enabling and, in some cases, compelling local governments to provide care for the insane poor. Justified on humanitarian and scientific grounds a flourishing industry developed overnight, creating purpose-built institutions and schools of medical training for the care of the insane, but this heady idealism soon found itself run aground on the broader concerns of finance and structural inequality.

Asylums, initially built for the care of hundreds, swelled to accommodate thousands and were overwhelmed with 'incurables' for whom no treatment seemed to lead to their eventual emancipation and economic self-sufficiency. Meanwhile, government was forced to reconcile with spiralling rates of insanity, a vast rate of urban poverty and a plethora of new social ills wrought by industrialization generated unemployment. Relentless demands for accommodation, food and clothing led to spiralling costs in managing these new institutions which suffered from overworked staff and increasingly squalid conditions arising from budget shortfalls, whilst the lack of effective treatments for mental illness led to huge numbers of the long-term insane spending much of their lives shackled within the institutions' walls.

Madness in the Colonies

It was in this context of medical reform that Governor Arthur Phillip landed at Sydney Cove in 1788 with a royal commission to 'entrust you with the care and commitment of the custody of said lunatiks and their estates and Wee do by these present give and grant unto you full power and authority without expecting any special warrant from Us.' (Bostock, 1968, 68) With the arrival of the first fleet, the baggage of European notions of madness and medical treatment were transported to Australia. The doctors and ships surgeons who treated the maladies of the crew on their long seven-month journey from England were part of a long-established pattern of transportation. The system was designed to deal with the overflow of the poor and disenfranchised who had rapidly filled English prisons and its deteriorating hulks in the wake of industrialization. Dunk argues that the inherent paradox of the colonial endeavour, to create a prosperous successful colony while constructing it as a site of terror across the empire, served to create a unique point of anxiety that promoted madness. When new convicts arrived at Botany Bay, they were confronted with the site of corpses in gibbets hanging in the harbour, a culture of brutal forced labour and common use of the lash. Under recommendations from Governor Bigges, the number of lashes was raised to over a hundred per flogging. Brutal apparatus from the workhouses of England were imported, such as the pillory and treadmill, blending the calculated breaking down of the spirit designed into nineteenth century penal institutions with the visceral gore and brutality of centuries earlier. (Dunk, 2019, 17)

The grand experiment of colonial transportation to Botany Bay was a unique response to the rising numbers of prisoners in British gaols and an increasingly fragmenting social order in England. While transportation had long been practiced in the Americas, the ambition of the first fleet represented a vast global redistribution of labour and colonization. In the early days of settlement in the colony of New South Wales, the primary focus was on the dual overriding issues of establishing a colony and sustaining the punishment of its predominantly convict population. There was an awareness of mental illness and a lip service approach to the care of the mentally ill but this was driven by the notion of work and discipline as the basis of mental health and as a cure to the ills wrought by idleness. Viscount Sydney, the architect of this colonial endeavour, hoped that the project would instil morality and industry in the prison population. (Dunk, 2019, 82) The insane were not a primary concern and, for the most part, if recognized, were confined within the prison system. In practice the colonial outpost was fundamentally a site of punishment and coercion. Illness and insanity were rife and the Principle Superintendent of convicts, William Hutchinson, argued that these could be as much an opportunity to escape forced labour and the lash. Many convicts were reported as seeking to feign illness and madness. Henry Graham, a surgeon at Norfolk Island commented that 'I know it is a practice among some prisoners to feign insanity for the purpose of evading punishment.' Often this 'madness' was manifested in violence, given the popular impression that 'real madness' was characterised by violent conduct and vociferous language. (Dunk, 2019, 87)

There was no asylum in the early colonial history of Australia. Those deemed insane were incarcerated in gaols and a variety of makeshift arrangements. In one case, James Ascott, deemed insane was left chained to a former ship's cannon for a considerable period. (Dunk, 2019, 6) This was all the more striking given the British Navy expected and planned for madness as a matter of policy, with sailors recorded as experiencing madness at seven times the normal rates of the general population due to regular head injuries, shock of gunfire, isolation and inebriation on dubious qualities of alcohol. Yet, by and large, little was done to accommodate rising numbers of the mentally ill for the first 20 years of the colony.

The earliest recorded committal was in 1805. It involved the convening of a jury of twelve and placed the property of 'Charles Bishop, Lunatick' in the hands of trustees to pay for the cost of his incarceration. Bishop was a navigator and trading partner of the explorer George Bass, with experience trading between Cape Colony and China. As a successful trader and free settler he had established what was regarded as a beautiful farm and property in the woods a few miles from Sydney. While having shown signs of being mentally unwell for some time, the death of his former friend and business partner, Bass, left Bishop distraught and too disruptive to live under the care of friends. A jury of twelve declared he was of an unfit mind to be able to care for himself and was incarcerated within a section of the Paramatta Gaol marked for the care of the insane. Having been declared mentally unsound, Bishop's property was taken by trustees to pay for his care and upkeep by the Governor.

> Now I, PHILIP GIDLEY KING Esquire, Governor as aforesaid, by virtue of the Power vested in me as aforesaid, do hereby commit the safe custody of the said Charles Bishop, Lunatick, together with such chattels, lands, and tenements as he may be possessed of in this Territory, unto John Mc'Arthur Esquire, and the Reverend Samuel Marsden, Clerk (they having voluntarily accepted the same from motives of humanity); hereby authorising and empowering them to make such provision out of the Estate of the said Lunatick as they may deem expedient for his maintenance and support, and moreover to do and act in all things for the benefit and advantage of the said Lunatick's Estates, of whatsoever kind or nature the same may be: and also to receive all monies, effects, and all other property whatsoever that may be due and owing or belonging to the said Lunatick's Estates; and to pay and discharge all such debts and demands as may be legally established before the several Courts of Judicature in this Territory, rendering me an account of the same whenever required and directed so to do. (Dunk, 2019)

In 1810, this procedure for declaring someone insane was streamlined from requiring a jury to only requiring a board of three surgeons, further bringing the determination of insanity under the control of the state. In recognition of the desirability of separating the mentally ill from the general prison and convict population, and to facilitate the search for appropriate facilities to house the growing population of people deemed mentally ill in the newly formed colony, the first asylum was established in 1811 under orders from Governor Lachlan MacQuarrie at Castle Hill in a former barn/barracks that could accommodate roughly twenty patients. It was run by a botanist and by doctors of various levels of medical training who had been sentenced as convicts, and was initially described in extremely favourable terms in the *Sydney Gazette*.

> His excellency, commiserating the unhappy condition of persons labouring under the affliction of mental derangement, has been pleased to order an asylum to be prepared for their reception at Castle Hill, whither they have been accordingly removed from their former place of confinement which was in the town gaol of Parramatta and every provision that humanity could suggest has been made for their accommodation and comfort. (Parkinson, 1981, 319–22)

Despite the glowing rhetoric this asylum soon became overcrowded and provided, even for a convict colony, such a horrendous lack of care in a grossly inadequate building that some suffered from extreme despair. It was closed in 1825 following a judicial inquiry which found the conditions grossly inadequate and called for newer purpose-built facilities.

> The Inquest further direct the consideration of the Court to the present extreme state of dilapidation of the Lunatic Asylum at Castle-hill, which (although its distance from Parramatta has prevented their actual visit to it) has been represented to them by the Surgeon, whose duty it is to attend it.
>
> Of the building itself, truly little need be said; its want of judicious subdivision originally, into strong cells or rooms

> for the necessary separation of persons extremely deranged, and violently disposed, from those of pacific harmless dispositions, added to its present ruinous condition, shew the absolute insufficiency of the whole to ensure the keeping, or administer in the least, to the personal comfort of its insane inmates, whose numbers at this period amount to forty.
>
> The number of attendants, at this Asylum, is also reported to the Inquest to be by no means sufficient for the attention required by some of the lunatics, and with this consideration, the Inquest suggest the necessity of the erection of a building adapted to the important purpose of due care of those unfortunate persons in a more eligible situation nearer the town. (*Sydney Gazette*, 3.3.1825, 3)

A renovated court-house in Liverpool was subsequently utilised for care of the insane until 1838 when the first purpose-built asylum was erected at Tarban Creek in Sydney, at Bedlam point on the Paramatta River, the site of what is now Gladesville Hospital. This asylum for the colony of New South Wales also served as the asylum for the new colony of Port Phillip, later to be known as the colony of Victoria. Despite its official role the enormous distances represented and the unreliability of transport between the two colonies meant that most of the Port Phillip patients were cared for in stop-gap arrangements such as a thatched slab hut in Spencer Street Melbourne, a home belonging to John Batman and the Lunacy Ward attached to the Collins St West Gaol. (Brothers, 1957, 11) Nonetheless, Tarban Creek became the working model for asylums across the country with its procedures and institutional models replicated in most early asylums in Australia. (Bonwick, 1996, 29)

Tarban Creek Asylum itself was initially run by the attendant Joseph Digby, a former employee of St Luke's Hospital in London. Though not medically trained, he had absolute control of the asylum and was an advocate of Pinel's Moral Treatment plan for the insane. Under the advice of the new superintendent Dr Campbell, the goal was to follow Pinel's principles of Moral Treatment while maintaining older models of restraints and disciplines as 'an active part of the treatment armamentarium.' (Monk, 2008, 32) Attendants were under instructions to prevent violence and calm patients who were likely to become excitable. Monk argued this showed a focus on encouraging attendants to work with patients on controlling their madness. As an example she sites the rules surrounding meals; attendants were requested to watch over the patients and meals were never to be hurried over or eaten without due decorum and manners. The attendants were, in theory, to be watchful and protect the insane from each other; they were to be kind in conduct and speech and never threaten or strike patients, and to always be neat and well presented. (Monk, 2008, 33) In practice such policies were difficult to enforce and a pattern of conflict between medical staff, attendants and other local authorities became entrenched in the asylum system despite numerous attempts at reform.

These regulations were reviewed in 1848 and in theory set out a system of accountability for attendants who were subject to the control of a superintendent. The superintendent was to be responsible for discipline, hygiene and medical care. He would visit with the patients regularly and ensure that the staff were enacting the appropriate level of care and seeing that the patients were off to sleep at night. (Monk, 2008, 33) In theory, superintendents had enormous power over their institutions in line with practices established at Colney Hatch and other British institutions but in practice, the early nineteenth century model of asylums was extremely complicated and the funding bodies and local apparatus of government routinely worked at restricting the level of power and influence held by medical staff. Local magistrates maintained a strict control over the financing, supervision, and visitation of their asylums and hired and fired medical and other staff at their discretion. Asylum management also faced considerable interference from the colonial government. (Wright, 1997) In his research on the enormous asylum at Colney Hatch, Hunter argued that in many cases medical staff often had little control over admissions, rarely had any exchanges with patients before they were committed and were only able to advise on their discharge. (Hunter & Macalpine, 1974) At the Yarra

Bend Asylum this complex power structure was to lead to some of the first high profile scandals for the treatment of the insane in Victoria, and this will be discussed in the next chapter. Wright argues,

> Clearly, the medical profession waged an explicit campaign in various national contexts to enhance the authority of resident medical officers. But this campaign occurred at the same time, rather than prior to, the dramatic increase in patients; and the decentralized nature of most nineteenth-century states, where the establishment of purpose-built institutions was left to local authorities, inevitably undermined collective action. So medical superintendents in these countries could complain bitterly that they had little or no control over who was admitted to their asylums, and had little political clout to press their case effectively … (Wright, 1997)

Thus, apart from their roles in persuading a sceptical public about the therapeutic efficacy of medical treatment in an institutional setting, and their administrative roles in the process of certification – both of which will be discussed later in this book – medical superintendents were unable to influence significantly the process of confinement. It was a social phenomenon of dramatic proportions, seemingly outside their control. (Wright, 1997)

Despite the promising beginnings, fractures and scandal soon began to plague the burgeoning asylum system in Australia, leading to a Commission of Inquiry into the care and treatment of patients at the Tarban Creek Asylum in 1854. The commission found that overall standards at the Tarban Creek Asylum had fallen well short of expectations with patients suffering from overcrowding; delays in admission left many patients languishing in gaols, violent criminals were mixed within the general population and the patients showed overall signs of neglect and indifference from staff. (McDonald, 1971)

As was commented in the papers,

> In the latter days of Mr. Digby's administration, we know that an amount of profligacy and licentiousness was openly practised in the establishment, which led to the merited overthrow of a bad system infamously administered. If a patient, under the influence of active insanity, fell into the hands of the keepers, as a matter of course he would, in his uncontrolled madness, strike his keeper, or kick or plunge about. This was the signal for practising the 'lex talionis'. The insane patient was beaten or kicked by his heartless keeper; he was put in the strait-jacket, was chained in his cell, and was subjected to many other indignities which generally left him incurable – hence the small number of patients who were restored to their friends and to society under that cruel coercion system. (*Sydney Morning Herald*, 11.2.1857, 8)

Clearly a new approach was warranted, one which could accommodate the enormous rise of mental illness in the colonies of Australia which had so dramatically overloaded the Asylum at Tarban Creek, initially designed to accommodate sixty patients. This new approach was to utilize the best practice of Moral Treatment for patients in purpose built large asylums with beautiful surrounds, well trained staff and the best medical support the colonial government could supply. With this in mind, the colonial government of New South Wales orchestrated the building of a new asylum in the colony of Port Phillip, what was to become the Yarra Bend Asylum, the first of many.

The rapid deterioration of these new asylums raises the question of how it was that these institutions, built on the ideology of creating a therapeutic community and designed to alleviate the suffering caused by mental illness, could deteriorate so quickly into places of 'Dickensian madness'? How could a place created to be a humane and principled place of healing turn into a place of horror beset with scandals, inquiries, multiple deaths and an almost absolute abandonment of all that was dreamed of by its founders?

Carl Jung perceived that when we encounter phenomena such as this, such as we see in the huge disparity between the asylums' original ideals and the abject horror they actually generated, it is almost certain that there is in some sense a failure to recognize, acknowledge and face the shadow aspects of ourselves and it is this which creates such incongruity, not only at a personal level but also collectively. The inability of a society to acknowledge and own its shadow drives objectification, the process whereby the perception of the other as a person is lost because they are engulfed in the objectifying of their presence as an object of the observers anxiety, their denial of what they themselves might be or might become as an individual but even more so as a collective. The power of the collective shadow is immensely more powerful than the will of the individual and easily swamps the personal résistance and reason, sweeping the individual up in its power. Objectification fuels prejudices between groups and ignites wars between nations. It allows abuse and created hopelessness to thrive because the abused are not people, they are the objectification of the projected shadow. As Jung writes,

> The group experience takes place at a lower level of consciousness than the experience of an individual. This is due to the fact that, when many people gather together to share one common emotion, the total psyche emerging from the group is below the level of the individual psyche. If it is a very large group, the collective psyche will be more like the psyche of an animal, which is the reason why the ethical attitude of large organizations is always doubtful. The psychology of a large crowd inevitably sinks to the level of mob psychology. (Jung, 1981, para. 225)

3

A Time of Scandal

Yarra Bend and the Birth of Asylums in Victoria

> It therefore remains uncertain how the bruises and sores on the person of the deceased Mary Anne Huggett were brought about. It has not been shown whether they were self-inflicted, whether they were the result of any restraints used to coerce her, whether they were caused by ill-usage from other lunatics or Prisoners at the Western Gaol – or whether they were received after she left the gaol and before she entered the Asylum – or whether they resulted from any two or more of these causes combined. (*Argus*, 26.9.1859)

During the early nineteenth century there was little provision for the care of the insane in either Sydney or the Port Phillip District of the Colony of New South Wales, beyond the ad-hock arrangements within the gaol system and make-shift arrangements in various wattle and daub buildings. Gaols were very makeshift affairs known as 'lockups', a thatched slab building on Spencer Street, a wattle and daub hut on Collins Street which also served as an impromptu hospital. After the hut was burned to the ground by the Kulin people in 1837 a brick home on the corner of Flinders and Williams

Streets was utilised as a temporary asylum and gaol. It was replaced in 1838 with a small purpose-built gaol at the Western Market, along with a variety of other 'temporary' measures. Pressure for purpose-built facilities for the mentally ill began to grow, leading to public calls for a 'mad house' to be established rather than have lunatics imprisoned within the Collins Street Watch House, partly because of the increased demands this placed on Sydney but also because of the perceived disruption of housing the insane within audible range of the community.

> A Mad House. It is highly necessary that some building should be set apart for the reception of lunatics. At present, the New Watchhouse is appropriated for that purpose to the great annoyance of inhabitants in that vicinity who are nightly aroused from their slumbers by the maniacal yells of those who are there confined. (*Port Phillip Gazette*, 1.12.1841, 3)

Nonetheless, it was to be four years before an asylum with medical care and support would be built in the district of Port Phillip. While the insane were supposed to be transferred to the asylum in Tarban Creek, most ended up within the prison system without any specialised medical care and were integrated in confinement with other 'deviants' within the broader prison system. Those with more wealth might be able to afford private medical care but by and large the rest were, for the most part, viewed as criminals or vagrants. In 1847 there were fifteen men and women remanded as lunatics and held in prison at the Collin's Street Gaol but there was no means of ensuring their safety nor of segregating them from prisoners of the opposite sex. (Monk, 2008) It was also apparent that this number represented a tiny fraction of those suffering from insanity, the rest contained within gaols, workhouses or, in many cases, living as vagrants.

In the nineteenth century psychiatry had been enveloped by the notion of 'Moral Treatment' as the almost exclusive means of treating madness. Moral Treatment as proposed by William Tuke and Philippe Pinel, argued that the mad were not bad people to be punished but suffering humans who had erred and gone astray and who could be brought back to the right path through compassion, conversation and kindness. To this end, if admitted to an asylum for treatment there would be no physical restraints, no chains, belts and bags, nor would there be blood-letting and purging. Asylums were not built for the institutionalisation of people suffering from mental illness; they were, as the word asylum indicates, a sanctuary or retreat, and idealised as a therapeutic landscape. The purpose of asylums was to provide a place of shelter and protection for people suffering from what was known in the nineteenth century as madness, with the intention that the very environment itself would facilitate healing.

In 1845, a grant of £1,000 with an agreement final construction costs were not to exceed £3,000, was directed towards the building of a new lunatic asylum in Melbourne at Yarra Bend. The design was created to facilitate these principles and to accommodate Melbourne's rising European population. It became clear that the colony had vastly underestimated the costs of construction.

Lunatic Asylum

> The daily increasing necessity for the establishment of an asylum of this description, has at length forced itself upon the consideration of the government. The sum of £1,000 was awarded, for the promotion of this object by the last Appropriation Bill, and since that period a plan has been forwarded to the local executive, by which it would appear that the gross area of the building is to be two hundred and fifty feet by two hundred feet: The site fixed upon, is on the-Merri Creek, distant about three and a half miles from Melbourne. The estimated cost of this institution, in conformity with the plan, is somewhat about £6,000 (exclusive of the internal fittings up), and seeing that the Bill last alluded to, appropriates 'any sum or sums of money not

> exceeding one thousand pounds, towards building a Lunatic Asylum in the Port Phillip District, it being understood that the whole expense shall not exceed three thousand pounds, it is to be presumed that the dimensions of the plan will be curtailed, or that the Supplementary Estimate for 1846 will exhibit much more liberal evidences in support of our public works, than has hitherto been the case. (*Port Phillip Patriot and Morning Advertiser*, 7.4.1846, 2)

Nevertheless, construction continued unabated and within a few months calls went out for the position of superintendent and other staff. Originally it was known at the Lunatic Asylum: Merri Creek, a ward of Tarban Creek, but after separation between the colonies of Victoria and New South Wales it became known as the Yarra Bend Lunatic Asylum. As in the practice of British asylums, a structure was established whereby a layman would be employed as superintendent and a medical man appointed to visit and attend to the medical requirements of patients. A former military officer, George Watson was appointed as senior attendant with his wife Mary to act as Matron. Despite protestations from the *Argus* that there were other more qualified staff available, Governor La Trobe remained steadfast in his choice on the basis of Watson's past experience as a clerk at Tarban Creek. Dr Cussens was hired as visiting medical officer. His duties included,

> A full history of the case of every patient, detailing the symptoms and progress and treatment of the disease, at each visit when the disease is active; never giving a dose of medicine without stating the symptoms which indicates it; and twice at least in every month, noting in the Register the state of each patient in the Asylum. (Monk, 2008, 32)

He was also required to examine the bodies of deceased patients, detail their appearance and physical condition and to pay special attention to the condition of their brains, recording all this in the register. A process for referral was established, attempting to take a more medically oriented approach than had been previously practised, whereby a patient could only be admitted,

> 1: By Application of a friend together with two medical certificates, the petition being sanctioned by a judge of the supreme court, transmitted to the Governor who issues the necessary warrant, the patient being admitted accordingly.
>
> 2: The Insane person was given in charge to the Police. The Police furnished the necessary evidence to the Bench, who remanded the lunatic for one week, during which time he was examined by two medical practitioners. If found insane he was committed by warrant to the asylum and moved there when a vacancy occurred. (Brothers, 1957, 16)

This approach would, in theory, limit the admittance of patients to when it was medically appropriate and those admitting were required to sign an agreement where the two responsible persons would guarantee a payment for their upkeep of 1/4d per day. With paupers, a certificate was required by someone recognized as respectable by the government, to the effect that the person was without income or friends who could maintain them. For a person to be discharged it would be required for the colonial secretary to receive two certificates of sanity whereby the government would issue the formal order for release. In theory this would alleviate a lot of the irregularities that permitted the incarceration of inconvenient relatives or spouses. In practice, the application of the rules was considerably lax. Brothers notes that in practice most of the admissions were simply signed by Governor La Trobe, despite not being empowered to do so without medical certification. (Brothers, 1957, 19)

Attendants were also closely structured under this system and defined with a clear professional identity. They were required to observe patients carefully, to view the appetite and excretions of patients, the patients' habits and moods as well as the day to day care and hygiene of the asylum, and to report to the medical officer. The moral philosophy of Pinel was integrated into regulations; restraints were to be used as a last resort but were still retained as an active part of the treatment armamentarium. They were to be used to prevent violence and restrain the tempers of the patients while still attempting to follow the best principles of humane treatment. Attendants were to assist patients in restraining their madness and follow the mores of polite society. (Monk, 2008, 30) Yet for all this process and regulation, within four years, the Yarra Bend Asylum was engulfed in scandal.

> One would fancy that nothing would appeal more immediately to the sympathies of every really good man than the condition of the lunatic. It affords a remarkable clue to the real nature of our 'private character' Governor, that Mr. James Smith, the Visiting Justice, who, in the face of such atrocities, pronounces the Asylum one of the best managed establishments in the Colony, is one of his prime favourites, and a constituent of almost every board that ever yet sat upon any subject that Mr. Watson, the Superintendent, under whose management such evils have been winked at and encouraged, has already received a fresh appointment; and that Doctor Embling, a conscientious and intelligent man, through whose agency these abuses have mainly been exposed, has been dismissed or suspended from the public service, and turned adrift upon crowded Melbourne to seek shelter for his wife and family as he may. The poor broken-down lunatic is a fitting victim to be trampled on, trifled with, and neglected. He is helpless and friendless, and therefore unworthy of a second thought. And this, good people of Victoria, is the Government to which, for years past, you have been subjected! (*Argus*, 12.2.1853, 4)

In the early years of Yarra Bend, very little information was released on the conditions of the asylum. Brothers notes that as early as June of 1850, the lack of public information as to the conditions within and the running of the asylum was already an issue remarked upon in the press. As rumours and gossip began to mount within the community, parliamentarians Johnson and Ebden organized the appointment of a full-time medical professional to be employed at the asylum in addition to the visiting Colonial Surgeon. (Brothers, 1957, 21) Embling, a former visiting medical officer at Hanwell Asylum in Britain was amply qualified for the position and was, in theory, to be placed in control of the asylum and its staff as the resident medical expert. Yet despite this, confusion reigned regarding his specific area of oversight and he did not receive a formal description of his role within the institution. (Monk, 2008, 41) In this unique circumstance, Embling assumed his authority to be absolute over both the medical and general care of the asylum and its patients. This view clashed with the perception of the asylum's Superintendent, George Watson, who saw himself as the superior of the newly appointed Resident Medical Officer. As Monk argues, this situation profoundly challenged the existing arrangement; the medical staff divided in their moral and medical duties of care and rehabilitation. (Monk, 2008, 41) It was an inherent recipe for catastrophe in any organization.

From the very beginning Watson resented the intrusion of Dr Embling into the running of the asylum and, with the support of the Colonial Surgeon sought to exclude Dr Embling from his duties, initially encouraging him to live off site but then moving to hide the keys to the wards, his home and barring doors to prevent entry. Despite these attempts to prevent access, Embling saw enough to be appalled at the condition and treatment of the lunatics and, struggling against the culture of bullying and exclusion, went to Mr Johnson, his sponsor in parliament, to reveal what he had experienced. Word of the situation was already reaching the public and in April of 1852 the *Argus* was campaigning for reform and investigation of conditions at the Yarra Bend Asylum. By the end of July, under considerable public pressure, a Select Committee was appointed to take evidence as to the conditions and functioning of the asylum. Initially, the Colonial Secretary and Governor sought to discredit Embling, but as evidence mounted with the 1852 Committee of Enquiry, the committee findings and public sentiment made defence of the institution and Watson increasingly untenable.

What became very clear through the Enquiry's findings was that the conflict went beyond simple clashes of power and authority between senior staff members. Watson's view of patient care was firmly rooted in the older forms of treatment and relied on little more than the use of mechanical restraints and physical punishments for perceived insubordination and misbehaviour. Conversely, Embling's experience in Britain and his medical training followed Pinel's model of Moral Treatment and new developments pioneered by British reformers. Embling was appalled by the treatment of patients at Yarra Bend. His depiction of the asylum, as revealed graphically in the pages of the *Argus*, presented it as a place of horrors beyond belief, a Golgotha and a chamber of horrors. He reported seven or eight patients crammed to a cell with the criminally insane mixed within the general population of the helpless and vulnerable, patients neglected and left in restraint for days or turned out in poor weather for hours unsupervised in filthy exercise yards. He described regular beatings and, in one case, a woman with initially no signs of insanity, driven to madness and death by neglect and abuse and buried in a concealed unmarked grave. (*Argus*, 14.7.1853, 5) Cussens, the Colonial Surgeon, was found to have been engaged in 'immoral conduct with an unmarried female attendant and to have engaged in bullying towards Embling. (Bonwick, 1996, 36) In the committee's report, the shower bath had become a torture to be used on unruly patients along with beatings and indiscriminate use of restraints. Furthermore, the report discussed rampant sexual abuse and assault against patients.

> Where in the application of the straight jacket, scenes of the most disgusting character invariably occurred, the impropriety being further added to by the obscenity of the lunatic attendant who always endeavoured to render the proceedings as immoral as possible. (Brothers, 1957, 25)

In public statements to the *Argus*, Embling railed against the conditions and abuses inflicted upon the lunatics of Victoria. He lamented that while treatment requires activity and exercise, the pattern of abuse and confinement only created more insanity. He was tempted to resign but the knowledge he stood alone between victims and criminals (in which he included the attendants) forced him to remain. He could not, 'consign the lunatics of Victoria to hopeless suffering without one friend to shield them.' Interestingly, in the Commission of the Enquiry, some attendants sided with Embling against Watson despite the apparent solidarity between the attendants under Watson. Richardson and Miller, despite facing dismissal and criminal sanctions, worked with Embling to enforce new rules in one ward to improve the lot of patients. They corroborated Embling's testimony, commenting that they saw him trying to bring about better order and safety for the patients, allowing the patients to become 'more lively' and praised Embling's wish to return divine services for the patients. (Monk, 2008, 43)

Public outrage in the colony was growing under the dramatic pronouncements of Dr Embling and the findings of the Enquiry, once publicised after some delay, led to calls for major reform. Andrew Scull's research into the scandals associated with asylums suggested that this pattern of major scandal was tied to the push for reforms. Reformers in mental health represented previous approaches to mental health as mired in cruelty and superstition, and 'conjured up' images of horrific madhouse attendants chaining their victims like animals in cages, abusing them at the whim of sexual deviancy and sadism with 'treatments' born of medieval ignorance and savagery. Whiggish historical approaches celebrated the reforms as the triumph of reason and progress over superstition, cruelty and madness. Much of the drive and public support for reforms was generated by publicly revealed scandals discovered through legislative inquiries, and the graphic images presented to the public through the media, in a sense, served as propaganda to support reform projects. (Scull, 1993, 46, 83, 87)

The Pressure to Reform

The graphic and voyeuristic fixation and depictions of sexual abuse, neglect and physical abuse released in the papers played a strong role in pressuring authorities for major reforms in mental health care. As Monk argues, while the graphic depictions in these inquiries should not be dismissed, they should also not necessarily be accepted uncritically. The 1852 Select Committee Report on the management of the Yarra Bend Asylum was a document that occurred in the context of the pressure for reform and the medicalization of madness. As a result, she argues, much of the complexity of life within the asylum was occluded beneath a harrowing tale of heavily publicised abuse. (Monk, 2008, 45) In Monk's research the life within the asylum was complex with a variety of relationships between patients, staff and the institution. The attendants were divided into factions over their loyalties to Watson and Embling and some in open defiance of Watson's management corroborated Embling's complaints in the Committee proceedings. In particular, the negative representation of an attendant named O'Donovan as a foul-mouthed abuser and rapist was heavily supported by staff and well publicised through the media to the horrified public. Conversely, O'Donovan responded to these accusations by arguing for his own good, moral Christian character and impugned the morals of the attendants who testified against him. Ironically the *Argus* report, when released in full, described O'Donovan' as a 'half insane attendant' and Governor La Trobe as a villain who 'handed the poor lunatic over to the tender mercies of a Watson, an O'Donovan, a Sullivan and a Smith.' (Monk, 2008, 54) In response to the brutal findings of the report, an Argus editorial placed much of the blame on a simpler issue of inadequate oversight and governmental incompetence on the part of La Trobe.

> But, politically considered, it is the old story after all – only another phase of Governmental incompetency. Unhappily, in this case the results of that inveterate evil are more palpably exhibited, and more keenly felt, than in, perhaps, any other

department of Government; for here the most wretched class of human beings, those who most deserve our compassion, are visited with gratuitous additional miseries, because of their very helplessness; here vice is nurtured, depravity flourishes, petulation thrives, and inefficiency prospers, while honesty and manliness, and the desire to fulfil duty, are ignominiously flung out to perish.

In order to show the frightful evils that may spring from inefficiency in the head of a Government, let it be noted that all the scandalous facts exposed in the Report would have been averted by the appointment of an able and honest visitor for the Asylum. Such a person would never have permitted the gross delinquencies that passed unobserved under the watchful inspection of Mr. James Smith. But, from that gentleman's own evidence, it is clear that there could hardly have been found in the Colony a more unfit person for the appointment of Visiting Justice. He is utterly destitute of the one faculty necessary in such a functionary – that of observation. He would not see a hole in a ladder, if you did not carefully point it out to him, and put his hand upon it. He is not cognizant of a single circumstance calling for condemnatory remark. All that he knows is that it is an admirably-managed Institution; that he never heard any complaints; that he had nothing to do with the medical or moral management of the Asylum; that, in fact, he had nothing to do but to attend to certain rules, which rules had only been furnished to him very recently. His business was to go over the place once a fortnight, when not prevented by bad health, or flooded creeks, or anything of that kind and occasionally to sign a book he never read. This was the Visiting Justice; and we must say that Dogberry himself would have better filled the situation.

> But the fault was not the Visiting Justice's; he could not act according to instructions, simply because he never got any. (*Argus*, 21.2.1853, 4)

Yet, despite the mounting public pressure for reform, the appalling representation in the media and the condemnation of the Select Committee of 1852, there is little evidence that the conditions of Yarra Bend or the treatment methods for those accused of madness changed significantly in the Enquiry's immediate aftermath. In her research into colonial mental health, Sands argues that custodial institutional treatment for mental illness remained remarkably static despite public outcry and horrific representations in the press and popular culture. (Sands, 2009, 364) Once again, by the 1860s reports began to emerge in the press of abuses by lunatic attendants and the difficulty in finding qualified attendants of a high moral character for what was referred to as 'the most repulsive of jobs.' Furthermore, structural issues tied to the ostracization of mental illness continued to make the hiring of attendants difficult due to the extreme hardship of being semi incarcerated within the walls of the asylum in a high stress occupation for very little renumeration. (Sands, 2009) This was despite the new superintendent, Robert Bowie's strong focus on patient welfare and commitment to Pinel's Moral Treatment. He continually requested additional and better accommodation for patients, strove for a good supply of fresh fruit, milk and vegetables with the creation of a patient run garden and wrote to the colonial secretary on numerous occasions out of concern for the state of patients transported from the gaol. (Brothers, 1957, 42) But despite this, tensions began to emerge as the costs of managing the insane began to grow and numbers surged.

Once again these tensions developed into another series of public scandals and feuds between the new role of Medical Superintendent held by Dr Robert Bowie, and Victoria's Chief Medical Officer, William McCrea. By 1859 the *Argus* was referring to the analogous state of affairs existing at Yarra Bend. (Brothers, 1957, 61) This led to another Select Committee of Enquiry into conditions at the Yarra Bend Asylum. In particular, it argued that McCrea had reduced the quality of the diet to such an extent it had become injurious to patients. Furthermore, the Committee drew attention to a state of significant overcrowding. While the asylum had been originally designed for twenty-five full time patients it had become rapidly overcrowded, reaching over three hundred patients by 1857. Over five thousand pounds was put aside for the building of a new asylum but it was entirely spent on alterations and new buildings at Yarra Bend. Yet despite the expense, the pressure of so many new patients meant the extensions were temporary and partial solutions and represented a serious decline in quality. Makeshift wooden buildings and tents were used to accommodate patients while original cells were modified to accommodate more patients per room in the already overcrowded wards. (Bonwick, 1996, 38). In the words of the *Argus*,

> In the exaggerated and distorted representations of the proceedings in lunatic asylums, which we often meet in novels, we find nothing really more painful than the revelations disclosed in this trial, or anything so graphic and interesting as the plain and unvarnished statements of the witnesses. There are all the materials of the tales of horrors – cruelty even to death, gross negligence, filthiness, dishonesty, and lust. Add to these, glimpses of the human nature of the world outside the walls of the asylum, professional pedantries and jealousies, official neglect, and legislatorial pure blindness and ignorance, and we think we have a chapter furnished to us of life in Victoria in 1862 such as can scarcely be paralleled for interest and variety. It is a shocking reflection that in this era of civilization, in the very centre of one of the most intelligent and well-informed communities in the world, which has lavished money in the effort to relieve its distressed and unfortunate members, of whatever description, such a state of things should have existed in the asylum at the Yarra Bend as has been disclosed by the evidence at this trial. (*Argus*, 9.6.1862)

Yet for all the critique of McCrea's management, Bowie himself came under sustained criticism for the use of restraints and 'bagging' in opposition to the new methods of patient care. The technique of 'bagging or sacking', a device of Bowie's own design, in which a patient was restrained within a large canvas sack, drew significant public attention. Whilst initially employed only irregularly on an estimated 3% of patients, and initially designed to allow greater freedom in movement than chains and ropes (Giese, 2018, 68), the accusation began to emerge that it was used irresponsibly as a form of discipline and punishment for unruly patients. The vivid depiction presented by Dr Carr of his treatment while incarcerated at Yarra Bend, presented a vivid image of disgust and horror for the media.

> 'A strait-waistcoat, padlocked, with the hands behind, was placed on me in the first instance. It was put on in such a way as to create actual physical torture. Over that waistcoat was placed a bag.'
>
> 'Tell us more about the bag', says Wyatt – 'how was it put on, how did you feel?'
>
> 'It was composed of strong No. 1 canvas, impervious to water, which was passed over the feet, and slipped up the body, fitting closely, the hands having to be placed flat against the sides. The bag came close round my neck – so close, indeed, that even the bugs could not get ingress between the bag and the neck. I continually passed urine into the bag, and there it was next morning, accompanied sometimes with faecal matter. The head was not protected from vermin ... My own head was bitten all over with bugs and fleas'. (*Argus*, 13.12.1854)

Yet for all these drastic findings of neglect and abuse, the technique of bagging was praised by some, arguing that the blanket lined canvas bags were less intrusive than straps, handcuffs and strait-jackets as they allowed some movement and, being laced around the neck and foot, allowed patients in calmer states to move around through the day. In the long run, despite Bowie being vindicated by the commission, he was asked to step down to be replaced; 'Some professional gentleman from amongst the eminent in England in the treatment of Lunatics was required as the new superintendent.' (Brothers, 1957, 61–2)

Despite the official vindication the representation of the asylum in the public mind must have been appalling. The descriptions in the papers were graphic and seemed to evince the worst images of life in an asylum evocative of gothic literature and horror stories. To have two such inquiries within a few short years, entrenched in the public mindset the notoriety of asylums, the mentally ill and the infamous Yarra Bend.

The question as to why the decaying and dilapidated carcasses of psychiatric hospitals have been left to stand for decades without renovation or demolition is bound up with the reality that every such building has a story to tell of how it came to be in this condition, whether that story is myth, legend or factual reportage. These dilapidated and decaying hulks mirror the failure of the asylum system to provide what they were created to be, a safe therapeutic space and instead became the host for an inhumane and cruel system. When institutions become moribund, their focus shifts to the mechanics, the fabric, without clear and concrete focus, without ideal or spirit. They become a shell of what they could be. The life and vitality had gone out of the asylums and they were left moribund and dead, the empty, decaying buildings a powerful symbol of what happened to the spirit of the institutions.

Moral Treatment, its ideals and focus were destined to fail; it fell out of favour with those who were responsible for the funding and the populating of the asylums because they lacked the vision, the will, the understanding and the ideals needed to successfully pursue and expedite such lofty goals. By the end of the nineteenth century due to massive overcrowding, understaffing, the large number of uncured patients and the poor standard of given care, government and community had grown pessimistic about the efficacy of the notion of the therapeutic landscape. Moral Treatment within the asylum had deteriorated to such an extent that abuse and neglect had become commonplace and that enduring legacy has left us with the lasting image we have of asylums today, places to be feared and avoided, haunted spaces.

4

The Ararat Asylum

Gold Fever on Madman's Hill

> If there be any affliction to which human flesh is heir, that more than all others demands our common sympathy and support, it certainly is that of insanity. The worse than helpless state to which thousands of our fellow-creatures are annually reduced by the loss of their reasoning powers is sufficient to excite the most painful feelings in the minds of all who have the faintest glimmer of philanthropy in their composition. There is something so truly awful in the contemplation of a human being reduced to the level of the brute creation by a calamity to which each one of us is exposed – something so suggestive of the inestimable superiority of reason over instinct, in comparing the acts and impulses of a lunatic with those of a sane man – that it is impossible to regard the victims of so terrible an infliction but with feelings in which pity and awe are closely allied. (*Mt Alexander Mail*, 27.12.1864)

The discovery of gold in the small town of Clunes in 1851 led to a vast increase in population as people flocked to the burgeoning goldfields of Western Victoria. Even as early as 1853, over 120 ships arrived in in Melbourne with twelve thousand passengers in that year alone. (Giese, 2018, 5) More were landing in the ports of Geelong and Portland with others teeming across the border from New South Wales and South Australia. The discovery of gold generated the legend of a new world with boundless riches that could be picked up off the ground and this legend was heard by the credulous ears of the poor from the disenfranchised masses from poverty-stricken Ireland to the slums of London and Liverpool. The majority, at least initially, came pouring out from the poverty stricken of the British Isles, still reeling from the economic tumult wrought by the industrial revolution, potato famine and highland clearances. Others soon followed from war and flood ravaged southern China, the depleting goldfields of San Francisco and from as far away as Africa and Latin America. The Victorian Goldrush was truly a global migration on a nearly unprecedented scale. The population of a small frontier colony of Indigenous peoples, squatters and farm laborers suddenly became a rapidly expanding industrial colony with bustling metropolitan centers as the population swelled by hundreds of thousands in less than a few years.

For many the goldrush brought unparalleled wealth as diggers unearthed vast quantities of gold. Businesses sprang up overnight to aid the successful diggers in rapidly dispensing their newfound wealth. Saloons, retailers, restaurants, clothing stores, suppliers and a vast array of administrative infrastructure were built overnight to manage the newly found colony. Even the violent clashes between miners and troopers, culminating in the battle of Eureka Stockade did little to slow the vast pace of growth in the new colony of Victoria. In many cases the traditional social order of British aristocracy was turned on its head as miners suddenly achieved enormous wealth and influence while others with aristocratic and well-educated backgrounds might lose their fortune in days to ill-conceived investments. Melbourne along with regional centers like Ballarat, Castlemaine and Bendigo became thriving cities that strove to emulate the pomp and pageantry of Great Britain with spectacular architecture in bluestone and sandstone forming post-offices, grand cathedrals, government buildings and posh hotels. In the cultural melting pots of the goldfields anything could be had for a price. Within the Australian colonies, troopers dropped their batons, farmers left their fields and servants fled their homes to try their luck at digging for gold, much to the dismay of the British Colonial government struggling to maintain order as the population swelled.

For all the wealth, glamour and prospects of the Victorian goldfields, most did not make it. For many the expectations of a new El Dorado did not materialize and they were left with poverty and loss, no new world in which to create a bright and prosperous future. And there is another dark side to this history. The prosperity of the gold-rush was built on the land of the Indigenous peoples of Australia who were displaced, marginalized and almost destroyed under the weight of colonial occupation and environmental devastation. Likewise, despite the prominence of stories celebrating those who became wealthy and powerful on the goldfields of central Victoria, many who came to Ballarat during the Victorian era found themselves displaced and impoverished, facing disease, hunger, economic vulnerability, drawn into crime, prostitution and perilous working conditions. As much as the newspapers of the colony were filled with stories of miners who struck it rich they were also filled with stories of violent crime, sexual assault, brothels and children dying in scores from diphtheria, pox, typhus and murder, all the ills and suffering that come from poverty and chaos.

Colonial Victoria was from its very inception an immigrant community. After the discovery of gold, people from around the world came to central Victoria in the pursuit of gold and while gold mining remained the primary industry during the 1850s and 1860s a wide variety of businesses developed rapidly to support the mining industry with machinery, supplies, food, transport, entertainment and housing. The chaotic nature of this rapidly developing community, the attendant complexity in administering the colony and suppressing exploitation and police corruption led to a number of conflicts, of which the Eureka Stockade Rebellion is the most famous. There were also conflicts between ethnic communities, conflicts with the original Wauthaurong inhabitants and an enormous disparity between the rich and the poor, exacerbated by a lack of infrastructure in water, health care and policing. By the 1870s the industrial focus had shifted from alluvial gold to large scale deep lead mining and Ballarat rapidly began to industrialize with the advent of rail links to Melbourne and Geelong in 1866 and the establishment of telegraph lines. This led to another shift in population demographics as the fragmented networks of alluvial miners and small business entrepreneurs became absorbed into an industrial working class. Globalized links were formed with Britain and the United States but the inherent local ethnic diversity still remained with communities of Irish, Scandinavian, American, Chinese, Canadian and others still prominent in the local community.

As the numbers surged a new concern began to grow in the population, concern about lunacy and madness. Lunacy rates across Victoria were burgeoning and the asylums, already struggling with lack of resources and overcrowding, fractured under the weight of this new growth of madness, giving Victoria the title of 'the Maddest place on Earth'. (Giese, 2018, 7) Even the desperate desire to find gold and wealth was itself viewed as a kind of madness, utilizing phrases such as 'a mixed, ardent and excited population … their minds already half thrown off their balance by the glowing anticipations which attracted them.' (Nichols, MacKinnon and Reeves, 2007, 41) Madness was blamed on a host of causes, the proliferation of strong adulterated liquor and crass moonshine, an imagined hereditary tendency among the poor, masturbation, and poor moral character. Grief and disappointment were considered in educated discourse within the papers as was the chaos of life in the goldfields. Poverty and weakness were other contenders, these to be resolved through hard work and Christian teachings. Some argued that the problem arose out of the prevalence of families in Britain avoiding embarrassment by dispatching insane and difficult relatives to the colonies. But few clear answers were revealed. (Giese, 2018, 6–7) As discussed in the *Bendigo Advertiser*,

Our attention has been called to a marked and most distressing feature of colonial life, namely, the prevalence of lunacy, on the goldfields particularly... The *Argus*, in taking up the subject, seems to endorse this opinion. There can be no doubt that many cases of this description may be traced to intoxication and excessive indulgence of the sensual passions. But here, as in all other countries, there are other and less irradicable causes of madness. Ballarat does not stand alone in possessing a larger number of lunatics than seems proportionate to the aggregate number of its population. We need not stay to refer to statistics, for any one of lengthened experience on our mines must know that instances are to be met with almost every day.

Everyone, however, does not trouble himself to inquire what have been the inducements to insanity in each individual case that comes under his notice, and here we have no statistics to guide us. But this is what we really want in order to arrive at any practicable system for the prevention or suppression of this very serious malady. If we set every case down to the cause of intemperance, it comes to this, that forty-one excessively intemperate persons have met with their fate at Ballarat, besides a large number elsewhere, and all that can be done in the matter is to endeavor to legislate for the suppression of drunkenness, – a difficult matter, and one which has engaged the attention of the wisest and best men of all civilized nations for a considerable period. But we contend that drunkenness is not the only incentive to insanity in this colony, any more than anywhere else. We need not surely enter upon a detail of the many causes which do destroy the minds, and 'steal away the brains' of men. Misfortune and disappointment, which bruise and break the heart, – sickness and destitution, which sap and crush the physical powers, – these, and many other of 'the ills which

> flesh is heir to', contribute in even a greater degree perhaps than intemperance to the prostration of the mind.' (*Bendigo Advertiser*, 25.5.1857)

The article lays the cause of madness at the foot of the personal immoralities common on the goldfields, but there is no hint of perception in this that there may be a deeper disturbance that is working its way out into the common psyche. On the goldfields there was dislocation, displacement and pain in every quarter. The first nation people had been terribly dispossessed in a matter of a few short years. Janice Newton writes:

> The loss of over 50,000 Aboriginal lives resulted in three Select Inquiries and a Protection policy in the 1840s, laisser faire in the 1850s and a system of Missions and Reserves in the 1860s which tried to separate and remove Aborigines in the belief that they were dying out. By 1877 half of the known Aboriginal people were on Reserves and a central Victorian census listed only 38 aboriginal people living off reserves in the region (100 km radius from Ercildonne). By the mid-1880s, officially there were only 844 Aborigines left in the colony. (Newton, 2019, 64)

There was a profound displacement amongst the goldfields population; they had come from all around the world, leaving behind families, loved ones, cultures, communities, social networks, some brought unwillingly, some coerced, many with no concept of the norms and structures that were expected in this fledgling British colony. The corporate sense of disconnection and injustice to miners, to families, to the Indigenous people were profound and would have had immense affect upon people's state of mind. Yet, in the public mindset, as expressed in the *Argus*, the cause is alcohol, promiscuity, masturbation, misfortune and disappointment at 'not getting the gold.' The absences in this explanation are more illuminating than the diagnoses. Carl Jung argued that feelings and behaviours diagnosed as abnormal by the dominant culture are representative of the intrusion of unconscious material into the conscious mind. In contrast to the mainstream of a community, people suffering from psychosis are attempting to maintain continuity of meaning but the unconscious material they are dealing with is overwhelming their conscious mind and expresses itself in the form of delusions, psychosis and disconnection; they are expressing what is not able to be spoken and so it is expressed symbolically through madness; it is the madness out there that is being expressed in the internal world of the individual deemed 'mad'. 'What the artist and the insane have in common is common also to every human being – a restless creative fantasy that is constantly engaged in smoothing away the hard edges of reality'. (Jung, 1960, 177) For Jung, the breakdown of cognitive continuity that is characteristic of schizophrenia is a personalized vehicle for expressing that which is incongruous and discontinuous. For Jung, madness has meaning and the chaotic nature of the goldfields had much to do with the upsurge of what was termed madness.

Foucault argues that in western society the diagnosis of mental illness was one more means of control and the latest phase in the enactment of disciplinary power. (Foucault, 1967) This was not a new phenomenon but one that found various expressions through the ages. A similar dynamic might be seen at work, but expressed in a very different way, during the sixteenth century witch trials, a phenomena based on the dynamic of scapegoating and fictitious labeling as 'Other'. (Szaasz, 1961) The argument for the diagnosis and treatment of madness as a means of social control is supported by the icon of the creation of Aradale. A beautiful place, set on a hill, overlooking the madness, seeks to bring order and compliance but proves to be a beautiful façade obscuring abuse, pain, torture, exploitation and dehumanization. Inevitably, the task was going to be beyond the capacity of any government, because the reality had to find expression, and so it was that in a very short time, overcrowding and under-resourcing overtook the lofty goals laid out at Aradale's inception. Given the Jungian argument, it could never be anything else and its course was inevitable before the institution was begun.

As overcrowding in the asylums escalated, increased pressure was placed on the system. Some patients were placed in gaols; accommodation within the community was considered, perhaps the first examples in Australia of community-based care. Yarra Bend had become an overcrowded network of rooms, tents and ad hoc arrangements. (Bonwick, 1996, 37) In 1854 McCrea advocated the building of an entirely new asylum at Kew, based on the latest Colney Hatch model in England and advocating the best of Pinel's Moral Treatment. It was to be built in a beautiful location catching the prevailing winds. McCrae was a strong advocate of developing large scale barracks-based asylums of the British model in Australia to deal with the rising numbers of the insane, a desire Bonwick viewed as 'an almost mindless wish to transport the British system to Melbourne'. (Bonwick, 1996, 38) The debate was particularly pertinent given the dispersed nature of the goldrush, with rapidly growing regional cities such as Ballarat, Bendigo, Castlemaine, Ararat and Beechworth exploding across the state as population centers rose and fell with the varied fortunes of gold mining.

A New Era?

The 1863 the Victorian Lunatic Commission chose Ararat as the site for one of the two large regional asylums to be built in Victoria. While Ballarat was considered, Ararat was chosen as it was further from Melbourne and could serve as a center for western Victoria whereas patients from Ballarat could be easily transported either east or west by rail. Similarly, as gold began to decline in the region it was thought the £60,000 and associated labour required to erect the new asylum would serve as a stimulus to the local economy and help maintain employment, as it did for the next one hundred and thirty years. The site was chosen on a reserve of 267 acres of land on Flint Hill, later renamed Madman's Hill, which overlooked the town of Ararat. It was a splendid building of the Italianate style with large gardens and featuring the latest designs from the Colney Hatch and Kirkbride models of asylums. Despite legal conflicts over contracting in the building of the asylum, it opened in October of 1867 vastly over budget, at over £128,000. (Brothers, 1951, 86) The initial discussions about the Ararat Lunatic Asylum featured glowing commendation for the building's sophistication of design, self-sufficiency and ingeniousness that would surely create an ideal environment in which to care for the mentally ill and avoid the chaos of Bedlam. In the pages of the *Argus*:

> The place chosen for the Ararat asylum is, or rather was, a small cone-shaped hill, which possesses a gentle ascent from the westward, and stretches away in the opposite direction in a broad plateau, broken by slightly rolling ground interspersed with thinly growing eucalypti and shrubs to the base of the surrounding hills, which shelter the position. The barrier of the Pyrenees Ranges runs along the northward, while an irregular chain of the same hills breaks the view to the east, with those rugged mountains which add so much of picturesque effect to the situation of the town and the surrounding country. Southerly, the land runs far and level to the plains country, which extends for miles, in a series of prairie stretches and large salt lakes, towards the sea. Westerly, a spur of ranges extends north and south, and breaks the view on that side. The apex of the hill on which the building stands has been cut away, to permit of a sufficient level for the requirements of the asylum and for garden purposes, while the excavations so made allow of the erection of a sunken wall, which will effectually confine the patients without being visible from the inside, and thus preserve them from a sense of imprisonment.
>
> In approaching the building from any side, one can scarcely fail being impressed with the size and character of the structure. The style is Italian, and the apparently irregular outlines of the whole at once take away that barrack impression which is so often conveyed by buildings of a similar character.

The abutting wings and towers lend a pleasant effect, while the tall scattered chimneys which spring from the roof bestow a sense of comfort and pleasant habitableness to the place, which was evidently regarded by the architects as one of the most important features in their design. The aspect of the hospital is south-easterly, and on this side the front elevation is very imposing, depending for its effect upon general outline and broad masses of light and shade rather than ornamental detail. There is an almost entire absence of architectural ornamentation, except such as is absolutely requisite to take from the plainness of the front and point to the object of the designers. The entrance is by a spacious carriage gateway, above which run the galleries from the surgeon's quarters all around the building; on the one side are the public offices, and on the other the wards for the patients. These offices are spacious and in keeping with the character of the edifice, and connect conveniently with the other portions of the interior. The situation of the hospital might be described as that of a partial quadrangle broken by abutments, while in the centre of the space stands the portion devoted to the indoor amusement of the patients, and the cooking and washing of the whole establishment. Entering this part of the institution first, we are conducted up a flight of stone stairs to a number of apartments, where are the billiard-room (lighted from the roof), and the library, school, and anteroom. Looking down from the anteroom, the large hall is seen to advantage, which can be used as a dining room, a theater, or a ball-room, as occasion requires; at the northern end a raised gallery for musicians is erected, so that the orchestra will be completely separated from the dancers. This hall is seventy feet in length, twenty-six feet wide, and twenty-five feet high. It will be pleasingly ornamented with pilasters and other architectural devices.

At the end of the hall is an apartment, from whence the attendants will supply the table; and further in the same direction is the kitchen, with its immense fireplace for the cooking range. This apartment is about twenty-six feet square; and adjoining is a system of cellarage and stores on the same level, but excavated from the slope of the ground; the walls are of bluestone, and the cellars, as may be expected, perfectly cool in Summer. Near to this are the wash-house and drying-room, the entrance to the latter being through a double-iron door, which is needed for purposes of protection, as the plan of clothes-drying which will be carried on requires that this part of the establishment should be protected from the heat and steam.

Entering the main building, the visitor is conducted to the quarters of the officers, and the wards and day rooms of the patients. These consist almost entirely of a series of galleries, at one end of which are the rooms of the attendants; along the sides are built the apartments for the inmates, opening into the galleries and leading into the day rooms, where patients may amuse or employ themselves, according to the rules of the establishment. The galleries will be furnished with earth-closets and bath-rooms, and every convenience which the necessities of the patients can suggest. Some of the sleeping rooms are boarded for a considerable height, and otherwise protected by a kind of double shutter which closes upon the window with the least exertion, and effectually guards it from damage. At the end of the galleries are associated dormitories, where, as the name signifies, a number of the patients can sleep together. This nightly companionship, however, will only be granted to the least refractory of the inmates, and to those who can be allowed such an indulgence, the system has been found most beneficial in its results. It is worthy of remark that all the apartments are double floored and

> pugged, and thus the sounds in one ward cannot be conveyed either to those adjoining or to those below.
>
> The sounds are confined by the laying down of a species of mortar between the flooring, so that even inside a sense of order and repose will be preserved, which is not usually associated with the idea of 'Bedlam'. Within the space of a short article it is impossible to give a detailed description of the various rooms and wards, and the several admirable appliances which have been created for the wants and comforts of the patients; the result of a single visit is perfectly bewildering to one who is not intimately acquainted with building and architecture: yet the feeling which remains, nevertheless, is one of admiration at the talent exhibited in the plan, and at the perfect system of ventilation and lighting which pervades the whole establishment … (*Argus*, 14.12.1866)

1867 was a watershed year for the care of the insane in the colony of Victoria. Not only were two enormous new lunatic asylums built but the lunacy acts of 1867 brought forward wide sweeping reforms and legal structures for the treatment of the insane. For the first time, a lunacy department was developed, charged with managing the insane in the colony. The 1867 Lunacy Act also, for the first time, gave clear legal guidelines for those who were brought under the care of the new department in the asylum system. It defined 'lunatic' 'to mean any person, idiot or lunatic of unsound mind and incapable of managing himself or his affairs and whether found a lunatic by inquisition or not.' This broadened the definition of madness to include people with intellectual disabilities defined by the common nineteenth century labels as 'idiots' and 'imbeciles' and a wide array of other behavioral and 'deviant' issues among the population. (Fox, 2002, 146) Yet despite these apparent reforms, the ease with which a person could be declared a lunatic and incarcerated let to a wide spread outcry that many patients were declared insane purely as a reason that people considered them an embarrassment or burden who could be 'got rid of' or dispensed with, especially women who were pregnant out of wedlock, or married to men wishing to remarry. (Report from the board appointed to inquire into matters relating to the Kew Lunatic Asylum, 1876) Giese comments that the changes to the new lunacy laws led to Victoria's asylums becoming rapidly overcrowded with 'idiots', 'imbecile' children and people with other disabilities as well as those facing senility without hope of release. 'Wholly unoffending in their habits, weak in mind, and feeble in body, they need shelter and support indeed, but not in the costly care of the asylum'. (Giese, 2018, 51)

While this was a common feature in the papers and certainly a common plot device in gothic and romantic fiction from the era, it was perhaps most vividly presented to the public in the 'Sacking of a Wife' incident in which a woman was seized by her husband, a hotelier from Cape Schank and his police constable associate, bound and bagged and placed in a cart which was sent to the Yarra Bend Asylum to have her declared a lunatic. Upon arrival she was feverish, ill and trapped in her own excrement but had the good fortune to convince a medical doctor she was not insane but rather the victim of a plot to avoid payment of maintenance by her husband. Vividly depicted in the papers with illustrations, this article struck a nerve in the mind of the public already concerned about abuses within the system and still reeling from the revelations of recent scandalous commissions into abuse in asylum care.

> The defendant was the proprietor of a hotel at a distance of several miles from his present residence, and was formerly the licensee of the house. He was in the habit of leaving his house on Sundays and going to that house, from which he did not return until Monday. On his return some time since he brought a constable with him, and then sowed his wife up in a sack and put her into a cart and took her to Dromana. From there she was driven, in charge of the constable, to the Yarra Bend Asylum, under a warrant issued by Mr. Anderson, on a charge of being a violent lunatic.

> She complained that during the journey the constable persisted in smoking in her face, and made her sick, in spite of her protests against his doing so. On her arrival in Melbourne a certificate as to her insanity was signed by Dr M'Crea and another medical man, and she was removed to the Yarra Bend. After being placed there she was ill with fever for three weeks, in consequence of the treatment to which she had been subjected. The surgeon at that asylum said that she was not insane, and that it was shameful that she should have been sent there, and when she recovered from the fever he discharged her, as she was not insane. She then went to her sister at Northcote, and having applied to her husband for her clothing and something towards her support without avail, She was compelled to summon him for maintenance. (*The Age,* 16.6.1877)

In his research into the administration of the Ararat Asylum, Crowther argues that a key feature of this period, and the entrenched issues within asylum care in Victoria, pertained to the administrative style of Edward Paly, the Inspector of Asylums, 1863–1883. As the Victorian asylum system expanded in the 1860s to encompass multiple enormous barracks asylums and thousands of patients, Paley, initially responsible for Yarra Bend, added to his responsibilities the management of the new asylums at Kew, Beechworth, Sunbury & Ararat as well as the new lunacy wards and receiving houses at Sandhurst (Bendigo), Castlemaine, Ballarat, Cremorne and Geelong. Crowther argues that the cumulative effect of this overstretching of administrative roles was that the Paley administration 'decayed until he was reduced to a state of bureaucratic inactivity'. Furthermore, he argues that the colonial Victorian situation regarding the treatment of the insane was a uniquely over centralized bureaucracy which, in practice, forced the director to be consumed with administrative trivia. The newly built Ararat Asylum was the first to which he attempted to apply himself and, despite his best efforts, he showed little capacity to assert significant control over the running of the asylum, even in the most basic of concerns such as the appointment and dismissal of staff. In essence, the model instigated by McCrea in lunacy reform was transplanted, essentially in its entirety from England, and was orchestrated to protect the bureaucratic structure against any intervention by prominent personalities and outside expertise. The resulting situation was one in which asylums were managed through a complex web of bureaucracy, opaque processes and competing personal and vested interests that hampered asylum reform. The sheer scale of the enterprise of managing the asylum system in Victoria across enormous distances, combined with his role as resident medical officer of Yarra Bend became overwhelming for McCrea. (Crowther, 2007) An investigation of the Ararat Asylum letter book in 1868, less than a year after the glamour and idealism of its opening, demonstrated rapidly deteriorating professional relationships between the steward, the medical superintendent and the male and female attendants to the point where staff were demanding transfers due to the toxic work environment and persistent bullying. (VPRS, 7455) A study of the outgoing correspondence of this period reveals serious concerns from staff regarding the quality of the food and facilities for patients. Multiple letters were sent discussing the 'inferior quality' of food supplied to the Ararat Asylum and that the suppliers were not meeting their conditions of contract. One such letter, dated the 28th of March 1876, commented that the food supplied was so poor and contaminated as to be unfit for horse feed. (VPRS, 7455) Paley responded to this concern by granting the Ararat Asylum more land. It was argued that by having patients engaged in farm activities the institution could become self-supporting. This response comes within the context of the dominant ideology, lauding the moral benefits of hard work and collaborates with the ideal of allowing the patients much needed activity outside, in line with Pinel's Moral Treatment. A dairy, vineyards and pigs were all to produce a source of income to supplement that generated by the production of wine. However, due to problems of dry soil and lack of access to water it was difficult to maintain significant production, nevertheless this philosophy persisted.

The Ararat Asylum was given shops for carpenters, bootmakers, tailors and other much needed maintenance professions. Sewing, laundry and mending were performed by female patients. (Brothers, 1951, 87)

Little of this workplace toxicity reached the press, yet increasingly, scandals reached the ears of the public through the 1860s and 1870s and undoubtedly word of mouth regarding conditions would have spread through the community. Likewise, discussion of the outbreak of typhus was reported upon regularly by the press as an important social concern. A report into the sanitary conditions at the asylum found severe problems of overcrowding, poor ventilation and a flaw in the water catchment system in which excrement hurled by patients onto the verandah roof, frequently contaminated the water supply. (Gresswell, 1991) As early as 1875, media coverage of the asylum had shifted from discussion of balls and the produce of the farm, to that of describing the site as 'miserable' and requiring extensive development and additional care and support for patients. (*Argus*, 15.12.1875) On several occasions there was public outrage as reports began to spread of murder between patients, allegations of abuse by staff and overall squalid conditions in the asylum. In the *Geelong Advertiser*, the experience of visiting the Ararat asylum was likened to 'reading a trashy French novel' in that whilst it filled the reader with horror there was a morbid fascination which prevents one from looking away. The journalist described an asylum that, while apparently well stocked, showed dull lifeless patients with thin leather mittens, restraints, lacerated faces and dull eyes. (*Geelong Advertiser*, 25.6.1874)

Once again overcrowding became a serious problem reported upon in the papers as the numbers of those incarcerated began to grow. In his report on Yarra Bend, Paley noted that with well over a thousand patients it had become the eighth largest asylum in the world alongside Colney Hatch, New York City and Clermont in France. The situation had become quite untenable, especially when one considers the respective populations to which these asylums catered. (Bonwick, 1996, 46) At this point Ararat Asylum had nearly 400 patients despite being designed to accommodate 300 at full capacity. To house the growing number of patients a variety of ad hoc measures included patients sleeping in the halls, tents and cottage hospital wards quickly adapted to manage the continuing overflow of patients. Despite this the asylum numbers continued to grow, only to be occasionally relieved by the transferring of patients to other similarly overcrowded accommodations. (Brothers, 1951, 87)

Newspaper reportage of the asylum routinely featured examples of patients who engaged in murders, violence and sexual assault. A key feature in these stories was a fascination with violence and particularly sexual violence against women, much as was displayed in the 1852 Yarra Bend Inquiry. Bonwick goes so far as to argue that long term, high functioning female patients were considered indispensable to the smooth operation of asylums as they provided desperately needed additional unpaid labour, they lowered negative reportage and the costs of maintenance and would assist in the care of other patients. He argues that this dependence was so great that asylum management were often loath to allow them to be released. (Bonwick, 1996: 62) This especially applied to women who were diagnosed with conditions such as moral insanity (sexual licentiousness) and alcoholism (dipsomania) and required little supervision from staff. As Bonwick comments, these patients were extremely unlikely to be released from asylums but were, ironically, the most capable of functioning in the broader community. (Bonwick, 1996, 62–5) As Swaine and Musgrove argue, there was a context to this incarceration of women which was closely tied to broader social perceptions of women and more specifically their reproductive capacity, as a commodity which needed to be closely guarded. When combined with class based interpretations of women's sexuality, the overwhelming burden of intervention and incarceration in asylums was born by the poor. Their role in the asylums, like the home, was to be domestic labour, reasserting traditional gendered roles. The female lunatic, especially those with 'moral insanity', threatened gendered norms and were configured as both a moral and physical threat to society which demanded incarceration. (Ashton & Wilson, 2014, 3–7)

A Scandal Emerges

Into all this came the sensational case of Matilda Cutler in 1883. She was released into her husband's custody after a period of two years at the Ararat Lunatic Asylum. After her release she went, with her husband's support, to the *Ballarat Star* and *Courier* and reported shocking examples of abuse which included regular beatings and lacerations, involuntary confinement, use of freezing water and restraints as punishment and the horrific tale of a woman who died as the result of a nurse ramming a metal spoon down her throat.

> The colonies have recently been horrified at the terrible allegations made by an ex patient of an Adelaide Lunatic Asylum against the officials of ill-treatment and brutality by the attendants to unfortunate beings in their charge. If what has been stated to our reporter by a recent inmate of the Ararat Lunatic Asylum is a tiny way near the truth, it would appear as though our own institutions were in no respects better than the similar ones in adjacent colonies. Late on Friday evening – last, two highly respected citizens of Ballarat called, at the Star office, and brought under the notice of the editor the case of a recently discharged inmate' of the Ararat' Lunatic Asylum, residing in Eyre street, who had some terrible stories to relate regarding the manner in which she alleged that patients were habitually treated there. A member of the staff was accordingly, told off to interview Mrs ___ the person referred to, on Saturday last. Our reporter found Mrs___ to be an intelligent looking female of apparently about 40 years of age. She seemed sensible and collected and told her terrible story without exhibiting any of that excitement which one would naturally expect to find in a woman who had only recently been discharged from a lunatic asylum and who might have had some grievances against the officials.

She prefaced her remarks by saying that she did not wish to make her statements public for her own benefit, as she could gain nothing by so doing; but she was imbued with the desire to do something to relieve the sufferings of those sisters she had left behind – sufferings which, she alleges, were caused by the inhumanity and brutality of some of the attendants. Mrs ___ wished it to be understood that none of her statements were supposed to implicate the matron or the medical superintendent both of whom she asserts, were as kind as could be expected but were hoodwinked by the officials under them. Mrs ____ prefers several distinct charges against some of the attendants (or female warders) in the refractory ward of the Ararat Lunatic Asylum, commencing with drunkenness, and ending with one which almost approaches a graver charge. Mrs ____ alleges that the patients are ill used daily from the time of getting up in the morning until they retire to bed at night. In the event of inmates not arising punctually at the appointed hour, she avers that they have been dragged out of their beds on to the floor by the hair or ears, The bath would appear to be the place where a great amount of cruelty is exercised. Mrs ____ alleges that the attendants have frequently used the towel racks and the bunches of keys which they carry about with them, to punish their charges. To use our informant's own words, 'They have drawn rivers of blood from me, and my body is covered with bruises caused by the blows from these weapons. Every morning, the screams and yells of patients were fearful to hear after the bell rang, and when the patients began to move. I have told the attendants when they were ill-treating me thus that when I once got out of the Asylum they had not seen the last of me. The brutality is something dreadful. I have seen the attendants knocking the patients about one over the other.'

Mrs ____ when asked by our reporter why the matron or the doctor did not interfere, or whether they did not notice the bruises on the patients bodies, asserted that she had, herself, on one occasion showed one case, that of an inmate named Mary S___n, to the doctor, but could not say what steps bad been taken in the matter. She moreover alleges that a patient after being ill treated was removed by the attendants into some place of seclusion, there to remain until after the matron or medical superintendent had gone the usual rounds, or until the marks bad disappeared. Mrs____ states that there is scarcely an inmate who undergoes the ordeal of the bath but is marked with bruises, and whose body is discoloured from the effects of the blows. When asked who did the mischief, Mrs ___ said 'The attendants do it; indeed, I have been beaten and throttled myself by (here she gave the name of an attendant), when in the act of cleaning.'

Another allegation made by Mrs ___ is that the allowance of brandy, eggs, etc to patients are in a wholesale manner converted by the attendants to their own use, and that the effect of this is that the latter are guilty of frequent acts of drunkenness. In her own case, she asserts that during her incarceration in the asylum, extending over a period of nearly three years, she received brandy and sago on five occasions during the first fortnight, and eggs during the last week of her confinement. In the interim, she received none of these articles, although her husband had been repeatedly informed that they were included in her diet and were regularly administered. Our informant also alleges that of about £5 worth of clothing which was sent to her by her relatives, she brought nothing away with her.

The food, it is alleged, was generally sent in badly cooked, was served in a dirty manner, and was not properly dished up. Another serious statement is that patients were frequently administered inordinately large doses of salt for the purpose of weakening them and rendering them less troublesome to manage. The salts were given in large pannicans, and in the event of a little being spilled, another dose, equally as large, was administered. In the event of a patient refusing to 'take' food, Mrs ____ alleges that two or three of the attendants would gather round, and whilst one held the nose of the refractory patient, the others would force the food down her throat.

We have so far dealt with merely general details, but Mrs ___ mentions one particular case, in which she alleges that the patient, a Mrs C___n, died from the effects of the ill treatment during the 'forcing' process. This person on one occasion declined taking food, and the usual treatment, it is said, was resorted to. The bowl of the spoon was rammed so far down the gullet that the spoon had to be forcibly withdrawn, and the withdrawal was followed by a terrible gush of blood. This woman died about five months ago. Mrs_ ___ names two female patients, a Mrs W___y and 'old Mrs A___d,' whose deaths, she believes, were the result of the terrible usage they underwent. Other charges of a more or less serious nature are made by Mrs ___. She gives as reason for the ill-treatment (and of the fact of its not having previously come to light), that the majority of the female inmates are the wives of labourers, and whose husbands have perhaps drifted away, not knowing – and, in some cases, perhaps, little caring – what was the fate of their unhappy spouses. The subject, however, is altogether too painful to be farther dwelt upon. (*Ballarat Star*, 4.6.1883)

The reports were heavily denied by Dr Armstrong of the Ararat Asylum (*Ballarat Star*, 8.6.1883) however, corroborations began to emerge leading to widespread criticism of the asylum and its management. In investigating this story, review of disciplinary action against staff during the period of Cutler's incarceration reveals a number of declarations of assaults, leaving marks on patients and, in one case a sexual assault. They also reveal large numbers of incidents of staff being intoxicated at work, passing out asleep in the gardens, halls and patient beds and wide-spread theft of alcohol. (VPARL, 1988–92) All of this speaks of a crisis of morale, overcrowding and overwork in the Ararat Asylum grounds. Matilda Cutler was certainly a patient over the period and it is worth noting that patient medical records described her as manic and that she was in restraints every day between eight to sixteen hours during her stay at the asylum, for tearing her bed clothes. (VPRS, 18300) whereas conversely the seclusion register lists her as being in seclusion for 8 hours daily (VPRS, 18137), so demonstrating a clear disparity between reportage and practice within the asylum system.

Research by Lee-Ann Monk into the institute at Yarra Bend also indicates large scale under-reporting of abusive practices through the Victorian asylum system. In particular, the loophole of necessary violence allowed staff a considerable leeway in practice compared to the goals of the Moral Treatment system and the expectations of attendants. By cross referencing medical records with those of staff disciplinary processes a much clearer notion of conduct by attendants can be ascertained. In particular, suspicious injuries such as regularly fractured and bruised ribs and arms may indicate problems which were unmentioned in staff disciplinary records. Monk's research indicates systemic structural issues pertaining to lack of training, inadequate resources and a culture of ignoring patient injuries. (Monk, 2007, 1–11) This is paralleled by Bonwick's previously mentioned research into the operation of the Yarra Bend Asylum where he documents a number of quite horrific practices in the early nineteenth century asylums, ranging through overt sexual abuse, systematic neglect, excessive use of restraints and ice water treatments to control patients. (Bonwick, 1996, 30–2; Sands, 2009, 364–71) Outbreaks of typhoid and other serious diseases at the Ararat Lunatic Asylum were found in reports to be predominantly due to fundamental structural issues wrought by overcrowding and lack of adequate facilities to accommodate sewerage. (Gresswell, 1891, 12) Even outside these examples of overt mistreatment, poor hygiene and abuse, there were endemic problems created by the asylum system itself. As was argued in the 1884 report into mental hospitals in Victoria,

> Members of parochial boards too frequently draw conclusions on this subject from hurried visits. They are satisfied if they can see clean wards and sufficiently clothed patients. But they do not realize the weary monotony of the patients' existence; their prolonged confinement to rooms, the clean bareness of which is in itself chilling and depressing; their scanty exercise in narrow yards, and the feeling of injustice which such treatment frequently engenders in the minds of those in whom disease has not altogether destroyed the power of reflection. (Zox, 1886; XLVIII)

The 1886 Royal Commission

Paley's retirement in 1883 allowed for yet another Commission into the treatment of the insane in Victoria, the 1886 Zox report. After such visible scandals the need for major reform for the treatment of the insane was widely recognized. A royal commission was appointed in 1884 led by Ephraim Zox, a prominent Jewish businessman and politician. The terms of reference were to enquire into the state and condition of Victoria's asylums and treatment for the insane. In their investigation they found numerous structural and social issues within the asylum system. As Zox comments,

> Under our present system the infirm and imbecile are under lock and key, and we treat people who are fit to be boarded out as if they were prisoners not worthy to be trusted at large. A doctor may rightly think that a patient who has nearly recovered, or who is semi-insane and harmless, is not fit to engage in the struggle for life. But all 'good and strong grounds' for the forcible detention having been removed,

> the time has arrived when the patient should be allowed to choose. And if he prefers to enjoy his sacred liberty, with all its risks and troubles, no door should bar his outlet. (Zox, 1886, 49)

The report, with its scathing critique of the asylum system under Paley was widely publicized and has become a critical document in understanding the tensions in the asylum system during the Victorian era. (Crowther, 2007) In particular it noted the problems whereby the inspector of asylums was also a manager of the Tender Board for those asylums, causing problems of overreach but also substantive conflicts of interests. Similarly, the commission found the large barracks-like model for asylums had very rapidly deteriorated to become almost indistinguishable from gaols in practice. There was far too little scrutiny in the process by which members of the public could be declared insane. Large numbers of errors had been made with regards to the responsibility of signing certificates of insanity and the responsibility, which should be of the gravest concern was treated far too lightly. Classification was said to be defective with newly arrived patients being sent immediately to refractory wards and new arrivals were often crowded with 'noisy, excitable, dirty lunatics, as well as idiots, dotards and imbeciles, and, of most concern little effort was made to separate the criminally and violent insane from the general population.' (Brothers, 1951, 141) One of the most significant responses to this was the establishment of J Ward, a repurpose of the Ararat Gaol into a temporary asylum for the criminally insane, a temporary measure which lasted over a century before its closure in 1992.

Saunders, an attendant at the Ararat Asylum argued that the doctors he worked with understood very little surrounding the treatment and management of the insane but also felt that if he raised this to the head of his department he 'may as well pack up my carpet bag'. Even Albert Baldwin, an attendant brought over from London by Paley personally claimed that, in his experience, the medical treatment of the insane was a 'great humbug and system of masterly inactivity'. (Crowther, 2007) Tucker, in his review of Paley's work in 1887 asserted that the Ararat Asylum had, by the late 1870s, become 'barracks like, cold and gloomy, and calculated to producing a depressing effect on patients'. (Tucker, 1887) Yet despite these scathing criticisms and public scandals, the *Ararat Advertiser* and locals reliant on the income and security the asylum gave were more forgiving in their response, claiming the coolness of the corridors were a relief from the summer heat, patients enjoyed the luxury of passivity and that the asylum was both soothing and gentle. (Crowther, 2007) What was clear from the report was that asylums now enjoyed a powerful position in the local economy, scandals notwithstanding, and that change was difficult to enact within such a structured system. (Monk, 2008) As Zox commented, regarding the success of cottage and boarding out models of community based care,

> While the evidence is overwhelmingly in favour of the cottage or village plan, it is too late now to speak with regret as to what we have done. We have costly barracks at Kew, Beechworth, and Ararat, and they must be utilized. (Zox, 1886, XLIII)

5

On a Soiled White Charger

Cunningham Dax and Post-war Asylum Reform

> 'I LOOK forward to the day when there will be no difference in people's minds between a mental hospital and any other sort of hospital.' This is the hope which dominates the work of Dr E. Cunningham Dax, who is leaving the superbly appointed mental hospital in Surrey, where he is Superintendent, to take up his work in Melbourne later this year.
>
> Dr Dax's approach to his work is like a breath of clean air blowing into a roomful of ghosts. (*Argus*, 20.6.1951)

The post war years saw scandal once again rock the asylum system in Victoria. After decades of neglect through two world wars and the depression, as early as 1946 serious concern began to mount regarding conditions within Victorian asylums. The Ararat asylum, now Ararat Mental Hospital, came under specific criticism as dilapidated, overcrowded and poorly managed. One article commented,

> EVIDENCE of the shocking conditions under which patients and staff are living at Victorian mental hospitals

> is given in the annual report for 1947 of the Department of Mental Hygiene, which was tabled in the Legislative Assembly yesterday. The report discloses that of the 8,180 patients treated at Victorian mental hospitals during the year, 449 died – 86 from pneumonia, bronchitis, or pleurisy.
>
> ARARAT MENTAL HOSPITAL:
>
> Great difficulty is being experienced in maintaining buildings in a decent state of repair ... the flooring in many wards is in very bad condition, and all that can be done is to patch the dangerous spots. The Public Works Department has been unable to get anyone to repair the worn stone steps of a stairway on which several patients and staff on several occasions have fallen. (*Argus*, 4.11.1946)

Even a decade later, this perspective was reinforced with even more dire warnings, as public pressure demanded increased investigation into the 1955 Stoller report that had captivated the public through newspapers and the newly available medium of television which brought images from asylums into people's homes for the first time.

> Dr Stoller said that Ararat Mental Hospital had in the past become 'a dumping ground for seniles and chronics.' Catering for 857 patients, including 50 men in the criminal ward, its original buildings dated back to 1880. He noted that many of the wards were obviously sleeping more patients than they were built for originally. As a result of the increased number of patients, kitchens were obviously too small, hopelessly inadequate, and appalling in some cases. Hygiene facilities also became inadequate, and some wards had one bath and shower for over 60 patients. One female ward, of 55 patients was an absolute firetrap.
>
> Two female T.B.'s had to be housed in a communicating glassed-in passageway, contravening all isolation rules. An

> old fibro building had been added to the female infirm ward, and it had no lavatory accommodation. The entire ward boasted only one bath and no shower. Maintenance of ward and facilities on the male side, as well as hygienic provisions, were mostly disgraceful.
>
> Among 50 men housed in the criminal mental ward only 23 were criminal mental patients. The ward was two miles from the main hospital in an old common gaol, the urgent abolition of which was urged in 1905. It was designed to take only 14 patients, and contained a kitchen which had been condemned.
>
> Dr Stoller said: 'This is a most undesirable [*sic*] center for mental patients.' He said the administrative accommodation was unsatisfactory. There was not even a separate lavatory for the women staff. No full-coma insulin treatment was done as treatment was being done at the Ararat Hospital, and little other psychiatric therapy. The dentist called only one day a month, and had to work in a make-shift room.
>
> This hospital suffers from being 'at the end of the line' as far as the Mental Hygiene Department is concerned. (*Argus*, 9.5.1951, 3)

Into all this came Cunningham Dax. He applied in 1951 for the position of Chairman of the Mental Hygiene Authority in Victoria. In part this was due to his concern that the National Health Service in England was eroding the power of the psychiatrist in mental health care. He had high hopes of working in a new area where he could continue to enjoy the previous authority he had been able to wield in England. He came from a deeply entrenched tradition in British asylum management where 'the superintendent was God!' (Robson, 2002) He engaged in a radical process of transformation and modernization of mental health in Victoria and has come to be regarded as the turning point in the modernization of health care in Australia. He was also a master of public relations and his capacity to represent the interests of the psychiatric profession through lobbying and use of the media was exceptional. He demonstrated a unique capacity to represent his vision of psychiatric reform to the public in a manner which made full use of all the tools of modern media. He positioned himself as a campaigner for modernization against ignorance, neglect and abuse on behalf of the patients and began an unprecedented level of reform in Victorian psychiatry. New buildings, treatments, facilities and resources were all radically transformed under Dax's modernization program. He was a psychiatric knight errant leading the charge against the forces of darkness and superstition.

In the history of Victoria's treatment of the mentally ill, Dr Eric Cunningham Dax appears as a central figure. He came with something of the image of the hero and knight-errant saviour of the ailing and embattled asylum system of Victoria, due as much to his vibrant personality as to his apparently successful professional history in the area of psychiatric institutions in England.

The knight errant image bespokes a wandering knight who has broken away from the world of his own origins and has set off on his own to right wrongs or assert his own chivalric ideals. It is a romantic image of a medieval era, an age long gone. He is the hero who is on a quest to fight the dragon, save the princess, find the treasure and ultimately, to find the Holy Grail. Jung writes,

> He is no hero who never met the dragon, or who, if he once saw it, declared afterwards that he saw nothing. Equally, only one who has risked the fight with the dragon and is not overcome by it wins the hoard, the 'treasure' hard to attain. (Jung, 1963, para. 756)

In this context the Holy Grail is the cure for mental illness, the end to the mad houses, the auguring in of new developments in mental health pharmaceuticals, electroconvulsive shock treatment, leucotomies and lobotomies. The Holy Grail also represents one who sacrifices themselves to the cause.

The main feat of the hero is to overcome the monster of darkness: it is the long hoped for and expected triumph of consciousness over the unconscious. (Jung, 1991, para. 284)

The dragon or darkness in question was the Dickensian conditions of the mental health hospitals in Victoria. Mental health treatment was an insignificant part of government, understaffed, having no realistic budget and the mentally ill, the staff who cared for them and the buildings they occupied were neglected and decaying. In 1949 the Director of Mental Hygiene, Dr Cataranich, had a little office in the treasury, a departmental secretary and a typist. In contrast to all this, the Superintendents ran the hospitals with unbridled and unscrutinised power. They lived in very comfortable if not opulent accommodation, their gardens were tended by patients and they worked around three to four hours a day and played frequent golf. (Bower, 1997, 111) Such inequity and power inevitably generates great secrecy and protectiveness. This was the world into which Dr Dax inserted his not inconsiderable personality and expertise.

Dax advocated an openness that was uncommon in the mental health industry. Before his arrival in Victoria his name was already known to government, mental health professionals and the public. He brought with him his reputation as a man of culture with modern outlook and progressive ideas. He was interested in art and had introduced art therapy to the Netherne Hospital, his previous appointment in England. He also brought with him the art of his patients at Netherne. Dax believed that art could be harnessed by science and he had expressed this in his book, Experimental Studies in Psychiatric Art (1953). The treatment regime of psychiatry would be reinforced by art therapy. Dax believed that along with art therapy, the surgical advancements of leucotomy (the cutting of white nerve fibres within the brain) and electroconvulsive shock therapy would calm patients and alleviate their symptoms.

But Dax was an outsider, from England; his ideas were seen as being ‘imported’ or ‘imposed’. Furthermore, his appointment to the Chair of the

Mental Health Authority was over the heads of at least two other people who later had to work with him, John Cade and Charles Brothers. The seeds of resentment were in place for Dax from the outset.

Prior to the arrival of Cunningham Dax, the asylum system in Victoria bore the hallmarks of Dickensian workhouses. While the social conditions of ordinary people had greatly improved since WWII, the asylum system was existing in a self-created subculture; the patients' clothing was inadequate, more qualified staff needed to be recruited to reduce the quantity of work per staff member, the buildings of the asylums were dilapidated and dirty with blocked toilets, no urinals, cracked and broken cisterns; the wards greatly needed to be renovated and patients needed storage space for their clothes; toilet paper had to be issued to avoid blocking up the drains with newspaper. The asylum system had its own nurses and psychiatrists who, despite improvement in education, training and social and living conditions, remained separate from the general medical and nursing environment and because of the geography and social isolation of their workplaces were usually located away from mainstream society. Many of the psychiatrists were housed within the asylum itself. (Carpenter, 1980, 134)

As a result of considerable pressure by the newspapers, in 1948 a public inquiry was held into the mental health system by 'The society for the Promotion of the Welfare of the Mentally Afflicted' (Victoria) due to public concern at the treatment of patients in Victoria's asylums. (*Argus*, 1955, 5–6) In the community there was a sense of secrecy regarding what went on in the asylums. Public scrutiny was denied and revelations that emerged from the enquiry had horrified the population and the government. A rescuer was needed and Dr Eric Cunningham Dax was recruited for the task. He emigrated to Melbourne to take up the position of Founding Chair of the newly established Mental Hygiene Authority of Victoria. The Authority was formed as a response to the Kennedy Report of 1950 which arose from the institution of the 1948 enquiry, highlighting the plight of the psychiatric patients.

With the appointment of Cunningham Dax, Mr George Fewster, the member of Parliament for Essendon opined that the state could now leave the past behind and look to the future in its care of the mentally ill. He said,

> Whatever may be said about dark ages of the past, I suggest that now is the time to look to the future, while making the past merely a steppingstone to better things. We should bear in mind that mental health patients, through no fault of their own, are deprived of their ability to become normal citizens. The state should do all in its power to give them relief. (Fewster, 1950, 1808)

Cunningham Dax graduated from St Mary's Hospital Medical School, London, and had clinical and medical research experience in a number of psychiatric hospitals in England. In 1939 he was appointed Deputy Superintendent and in 1941 Superintendent of the Netherne Hospital in Surrey. The Netherne Hospital was a large institution where most of the patients were regarded as having chronic and incurable mental illness. Cunningham Dax refused to accept this grim diagnosis on these patients and introduced art therapy in the clinical setting. He was concerned about the social stigma of mental illness and was active in trying to reduce it. To do this he encouraged openness between the asylum and the surrounding society. He writes,

> It is fundamental to good administration that information about the various psychiatric services should be given to those concerned, and since ultimately the responsibility for these services is to the public, they should be kept in touch with what is happening. To avoid fears and prejudices and to gain support a two-way transmission of information is essential. … Therefore, the visitors should be encouraged to come to see where the patients live and work and should visit within the

> living accommodation, rather than in special visitors rooms … There should be open days so the public are free to come and see both hospitals and clinics. (Dax, 1962, 84–5)

Cunningham Dax's arrival from Surrey in 1951 was a pivotal point in the history of psychiatry in the state of Victoria. He took up the position of the first chairman of the Mental Hygiene Authority and according to history the beginning of the transformation of Victoria's dilapidated and decaying asylums into communities. The psychiatrist and biographer Reginald Ellery pondered on the hopes and expectation on Dax to modernise and develop a decaying and dilapidated psychiatric system. He writes,

> The eyes of Victoria are now focused upon this mild-mannered man who left his art classes in an orderly asylum in Surrey to rectify the discrepancies and supply the deficiencies of half a century's inadequate administration of the State's lunacy department. Pious hopes are vested in him by those who watch him roll up his shirt sleeves and face his tasks. (Ellery, 1955, 234)

The pictorial image of this English gentleman with his Shakespearean accent, his shirt sleeves rolled up ready to scrub a decaying and grimy mental health system, reflects the high expectations of government, public, patients and their families. In his obituary Cunningham Dax was described thus:

> He had a larger than life persona and the influence to match. Tough, tenacious and politically savvy, he was tall, preposterously perpendicular, impeccably dressed, arrestingly courteous and spoke with the rounded diction of a Shakespearean accent. (Westmore, 2008, 167–71)

According to Cunningham Dax himself, he was appointed at a time when the conditions of patients, deterioration of buildings and lack of training for staff was such that,

> Few administrative bodies have been so fortunate as to be appointed at a time when there was so much to do that it was difficult not to make improvements, or when public sympathy and hope ran so high. (Dax, 1961, 9)

Interestingly, Cunningham Dax's time as chair of the Mental Hygiene Authority coincided with an increase in the power of the public mental health system and with improvement of facilities within the public system. There was also an increase in staff; when Dax arrived to take up his post in 1951 there were nine psychiatrist superintendents in the public hospital system. By 1960, these figures had increased to seventeen, fifteen other psychiatrists and twenty-four medical officers. (Dax, 1998, 105) Dax actively worked towards developing the status and professionalism of the service. This was also seen in the training and research he initiated which in turn led to the recruiting of highly qualified people for the Victorian Mental Health Service, further increasing the emphasis on qualifications in apportioning promotions and new appointments.

The first Diploma of Psychological Medicine in Victoria had been inaugurated by the University of Melbourne in 1936 and the Department of Psychology was established in 1946, also by the University of Melbourne but a Professorship of Psychiatry was not established until 1964. Nevertheless, prior to these events, private psychiatrists had established their own training courses. (Rubenstein & Rubenstein, 1997, 4) Better academic standing and advanced training became increasingly common, adding to the competitive edge in the employment market. Training increased the status of the appointees, bettered the conditions of the patients and produced an apparently improved system.

However, the developments and increased status initiated by Dax created antagonism from the private psychiatrists and from some figures in the Mental Hygiene Authority. The child psychiatrist Dr Winston Rickards, director of the Child Development Research Unit and the

Royal Children's Hospital in Melbourne, endeavoured to mediate between private psychiatrists and the Mental Hygiene Authority and this at a time when psychiatrists were trying define themselves as academically and professionally on a par with other medical professionals and the question of specialization and protection of the psychiatrist was being defined so that only medical personnel with appropriate qualifications could be so named.

The divisions and tensions in psychiatry created with the arrival of Cunningham Dax and the subsequent specialisation of psychiatry was a continuing difficulty. At this time in the history of psychiatry in Victoria there were two streams of psychiatrists. One was within the public service, the other were private practitioners. The public service psychiatrists often had no specialist psychiatric degrees while the private psychiatrists were medical doctors with thriving practices and honorary positions at the Melbourne, St Vincent's and Alfred Hospitals. The private psychiatrists showed little respect for the public psychiatrists who perceived themselves to be no match for the prestigious professionals and had no option but to suffer in silence. Dax's legacy was to uplift the public service psychiatrists' status but did not address the divisions between these and the private psychiatrists, nor was he able to accommodate or value the role of psychotherapy. He favoured medical intervention that would 'calm the patient', but there is a question as to what that might mean. If it means the person becomes more manageable, what then remains of creativity and generativity in the patient's life?

The Mental Hygiene Authority Act 1950 specified that there must be a Chairman with qualifications in psychiatry, a Deputy Chairman also with qualifications in psychiatry, and a lay administrative member. The Mental Hygiene Authority was to report directly to the Minister of Health and use the Public Works Department for approval of buildings and the Public Service Board for non-clinical staff appointments. This was a move to legitimate the public psychiatrists' professional standing. The successful applicants for the positions of Deputy Chair and Secretary of the Mental Hygiene Authority had all had previous experience in the field. Charles Brothers, appointed Deputy Chairman, had previously been the Director of Mental Hygiene in Tasmania. His role was to take responsibility for monitoring of staff and patient conditions in Victoria's mental health facilities. Eric Ebbs was appointed secretary to the Mental Hygiene Authority; this decision was based on Ebb's previous hospital experience as the Secretary of Health in the Health Department's Tuberculosis section.

Dax's role within the Mental Hygiene Authority (MHA) was to co-ordinate overall policies, planning and public relations and to negotiate with the Public Works Authority. Charles Brothers was responsible for recruiting staff in conjunction with the Public Service Board, supervising drugs and pharmacies, and monitoring the standards and treatments. Ebbs was responsible for the offices, hospital maintenance staff, kitchens, and patient clothing.

The MHA was to make provision for the improvement of services to those suffering mental illness and to develop strategies for the prevention of mental defect disorder and disease as well as to conduct research, arrange for accommodation of patients and provide out-patient clinics and hostels for the mentally ill who were well enough to live in the community. The MHA was also required to make recommendation for improvement to the facilities in which patients were housed and to recommend amendments to the Mental Hygiene Acts and Regulations as required. (Mental Hygiene Authority Act, 1950 section 10)

There was a sea-change happening in the way treatment for mental illness was to be handled, from a century previous, when 'mentally defective' persons, as they were so described,

> … were considered to be fit subjects for confinement and treatment in our penal institutions, but an enlightened community today considers that this is a subject which should be taken right out of the atmosphere and consideration of restraint and confinement behind bars. (VLA, 1950, 1736)

For mental health, the perceived necessity for constraint was diminished by the availability of new pharmaceutical drugs and the surgical treatments which Dax had used at Netherne such as electroconvulsive therapies and leucotomies. In 1951, a publication in the Medical Journal of Australia by Noak and Trautner advocated the role of lithium in the treatment of mania, based on research by the psychiatrist John Cade at Mont Park Hospital. (McPhee, 1995, 105) The use of the drug largactil (chlorpromazine) in hospitals from 1954 appeared to Cade to offer a miracle drug destined to change the whole of psychiatry. (Cade, 1979, 47) An advertisement for a drug called Cemalonl in the Australian Psychiatric Bulletin of 1959 claimed that this drug was as 'modern as a jet'. (Rubenstein and Rubenstein, 1997, 26) Psychiatric medicine within Australia was enjoying a climate of optimism and the focus on technology which characterised a national image for the future.

Cunningham Dax's legacy was achieved by the convergence of a number of factors. The system, as it was, was so terrible that almost anything would have been an improvement. But his approach to the task, engendering openness and collaborative decision-making at a time when there were huge strides forward both pharmaceutically and surgically, meant that the time was opportune for huge changes for the better. That said, his approach entrenched the pathologizing of mental illness as a physical problem to be treated medically but left little space for reflection upon what might lie behind a person's life and experiences that might contribute to their illness, and little space for the possibilities that appropriate psychotherapeutic practice may offer the patients. This legacy legitimized and promoted a primarily medical model for the treatment of those with mental illness; such a model is hugely dependent on pharmaceuticals and consequently so are the patients; it leaves the pharmaceutical companies in an extraordinarily powerful position. Further, it assumes something about the definition of mental illness, that it is to be pathologized. In this sense, the stigma has not yet been dissolved. Psychotherapy would offer that those circumstances in which mental illness is detonated are often reflective of aspects of the psyche which are hugely creative. To simply suppress, medically, the symptoms, is also to ignore the potential that lies buried within the shadow, and therefore to incarcerate something of human creativity for the sake of comfort and convenience. Carl Sagan writes: 'Imagination would often carry us to worlds that never were, but without it we go nowhere'. (Sagan, 1980, 23)

Without imagination, Cunningham Dax would never have been able to envisage the changes that were needed to bring the Victorian asylum system into a new era. Without that imagination and vision he could never have had the determination or courage to see his vision through in the face of profound opposition and antagonism. Nor would he have been able to sustain his focus in times of setbacks and failures, and yet, some of the treatments that he was proposing, disenfranchised their recipients of these very qualities. The irony is that for him, these patients were better. There has to be a criterion by which this term is arrived at, but the question remains as to who decides what that criterion is, and who establishes the value system that defines that criterion.

The Lithium Revolution

In the nineteenth century, lithium was commonly used to treat gout, epilepsy and cancer (Sneader, 2005, 53) but its use did not become widespread until after WWII. The Australian Psychiatrist John Cade is credited with introducing lithium to treat mania and bipolar disorder in 1949. He discovered that lithium helped patients quickly regain stability. Cade's interest in lithium had developed during WWII when he was a prisoner of war in Singapore at the notorious Changi POW camp. He and the other soldiers endured overcrowded conditions, malnutrition and diseases: malaria, dysentery, beriberi and pellagra to name a few. It was here in the POW camp that Cade noticed certain food and vitamin deficiencies impacted on the minds of certain prisoners. He noted, particularly, that Vitamin B deficiencies like beriberi and pellagra caused delusions and listlessness. After the war he continued to explore his interest in the links between nutrition and mental state. Working from the Bundoora Mental Hospital in Melbourne he began to collect urine samples from individuals suffering from depression, mania and schizophrenia. He wanted to see if secretions in their urine could be correlated to their symptoms.

There was at this time no theoretical base to work from, no means of sophisticated chemical analysis so he experimented by injecting urine samples into the abdominal cavities of guinea pigs, raising the dose until they died. He theorised that the urine of individuals suffering from mania proved lethal to the animals. He also proposed that a large dose of lithium tended to calm the animals; the lithium had a tranquilising effect. He discovered he could lie them on their backs and the normally active guinea pigs would lie placidly back and look up at him.

Needing to consolidate his findings with a human test subject, he injected himself with lithium so as to formally establish a safe dose before trying it out on patients suffering from mania. In 1949 he reported his findings through the Medical Journal of Australia, that all patients to whom he had given trial doses had made fast and dramatic improvements and that five of these patients who had been in and out of Bundoora for years had been allowed to go home. (Cade, 1949, 349–51) However, John Cade's early success was marred and in 1950 Cade abandoned his experiments with lithium. The therapeutic dose for lithium is dangerously close to the toxic dose and that year one of Cade's patients with a history of bipolar disorder for thirty years, died from lithium poisoning. In that same year the Danish Psychiatrist Morgan Schou was also working hard to have lithium accepted as a treatment for bipolar disorder. He and Paul Baastrup conducted a series of lithium experiments with tighter controls and these culminated in a double blind, placebo controlled clinical trial and concluded after the trial that 'lithium prevents both manic and depressive episodes. (Baastrup, 1970, 350)

These clinical trials, like Cade's observations and experiments, worked off the assumption that the most critical factor was finding a chemical, a treatment that would cure the illness, the mania, the depression. For this reason the focus was upon the use of chemical responses to the mental dysfunctions they were seeking to address. But this approach did not address the circumstances of the patients' lives that may have laid behind why they became ill. At Changi prison for instance, it was observable that vitamin deficiencies altered psycho-somatic responses, but not all people responded in the same way, physically or mentally. A person's capacity to endure and to respond to a stressor depends on many factors: the person's state of mind when they encounter the stressor, their sociology by which they interpret the stressor, their personality by which they perceive the nature of the stressor's power and its potential. The capacity of a human subject to interpret and reinterpret any stimulus depends hugely on their internal perceptions, and this is expressed both in behaviour and in psychosomatic responses. A vitamin deficiency, for instance, is not merely a matter of chemical interactions between diet, environment, metabolism and stressors, so to simply address a mental illness as a pathology needing chemical counterindication may be to merely reduce the symptoms that are expressive of an underlying psychological dysfunction which needs to be addressed. To address the matter chemically or surgically may do little to reprieve a problem that lies in the way reality is perceived, interpreted and handled.

Psychosurgery in Australia

In the post WWII period thousands of demobilized military personnel were returning from the battlegrounds and prisoner of war camps in Europe and the East. Along with these were a host of immigrants from around the world; four and a half million immigrants came to Australia in response to vigorous immigration initiatives by the Australian government under the slogan 'Populate or Perish.' Many of the returning military personnel were suffering from PTSD; many of these migrants had also suffered hardship and loss due to the war: loss of homes, friends and family members, loss of jobs and the notion that life might offer a secure and safe future. In the highly optimistic tone of post war society there was little emotional space for people to process the horrors and griefs that war had inflicted.

In 1947, Cunningham Dax published a book titled 'Modern Mental Treatment: A handbook for nurses.' in which he noted in optimistic tones,

> … With the changing public outlook on mental and nervous illness, we can look forward to a future in which mental

> hospitals will be re-organized and the nurses be concerned with treatment rather than custody. (Dax, 1947, 11)

This rather optimistic handbook served several purposes; it highlighted the confidence and value invested in modern treatments and it was an encouragement for more nurses to join the mental health nursing profession. Furthermore, it underlined the importance of reform in the mental health hospitals.

The new physical treatments transformed the public image of mental hospitals. They offered a concrete response to what was now being described in clinical terms. It is clear that there was a more complex process taking place in the way these treatments were represented. The predominant medications available until the advent of modern psychopharmacology in the mid-20th century were chloral and bromides, introduced in 1871, and paraldehyde and barbiturates, first used in 1882 and 1903 respectively. Other treatments introduced in the first decades of the 20th century included malaria treatment for general paralysis of the insane in 1929 and arsenical treatment for syphilis in 1930, and during the 1930s insulin shock and cardiazol were given intravenously to induce convulsions on the basis that schizophrenia and convulsive disorders were mutually exclusive.

There was a sense of optimism that chronic mental illness would be a thing of the past. In his paper, The Evolution of Community Psychiatry, Dax noted that everyone believed in the treatments, including the patients themselves; morale was high and there was overwhelming optimism. (Dax, 1992, 77) The physical treatments gave new hope; chronic mental illness and incarceration were terms from the past, overtaken by enthusiasm for rehabilitation and open wards; the railings were taken down, industrial occupations started in locally constructed buildings, the patients had their own vegetable allotments, organised their social clubs and cafeterias and everything was happening in a hurry to make up for lost time. (Dax, 1992, 24)

This new optimism was founded on the implementation of the new 'physical treatment', the introduction of drugs like cardiazol and azaman which produced multiple fits but these were seen as part of the stabilization process. People were determined that schizophrenia could be cured with this drastic type of treatment. Alongside the new drug regime in mental health was the use of drugs designed to induce prolonged sleep, administration of drugs to create an insulin coma, electroconvulsive therapy (ECT) which according to Cunningham Dax enabled the most chronically depressed patients to be discharged. Pre-frontal leucotomies were used frequently from the 1940s to the 1970s. The operation was developed by Egas Moniz, a Portuguese neurologist who was awarded a Noble Prize for Medicine and Physiology in 1949 for the development of the procedure. The intention of the surgery was to sever nerve endings in the frontal lobes and thalamus by injecting alcohol through two holes drilled in either side of the skull. The aim of the leucotomy was to interrupt the nerve endings to and from the frontal lobe of the brain, so reducing mental and behavioural disturbances. A side effect of this was to cause marked personality and cognitive changes, however these were seen as a necessary if unfortunate collateral.

The social context of early psychosurgery is intriguing. It was women who were historically the preferred subjects for a leucotomy because 'it is easier for them to assume the role of housewife' after the procedure. (Showalter, 1985, 210) It is interesting that in the textbook written by William Slater, 'An Introduction to physical methods of treatment in Psychiatry' that he notes psychosurgery is recommended for women suffering from depression due to the fact that 'she might be in an extremely difficult marriage with a 'psychopathic husband' and can't for other reasons leave the relationship. (Sargent & Slater, 1972, 210) This observation highlights the earlier question; what do we mean by mental health?

In Australia there is a lack of published material on the psychosurgical procedure of leucotomy. The records that are available are those of a clinical follow-up from 1973–1995 to a study of a group of Australian patients who underwent bilateral leucotomies for severe depression. (Sachdev & Sachdev, 2005, 478–85) During this follow up of the seventy six patients, after an average of fourteen and a half years, twenty four had died and six of these had committed suicide, but of the fifty two remaining patients some had improved, and others had made a significant recovery.

There is a great lack of research into psychosurgery, particularly in government funded procedures and the loss of medical records is significant. (White & McGee-Collett, 2016, 425–7) This lack of records in Australia is a consequence of Public Mental Health Services in Australia being managed independently by six state governments, each with its own historical mental health records which are protected by state privacy and record keeping legislation restricting access for up to one hundred years. Australian neurosurgeons and psychiatrists also publish very little in national and international journals (Edwards, 1997, 512–16) so in the absence of well-kept records, historians can only speculate as to the number and type of leucotomies and the results of the operations.

What we do know is that for Dax the prefrontal leucotomy opened a new approach in psychiatry and in his opinion produced results that had previously been unobtainable. In his opinion, its various techniques, clinical indications and therapeutic values had been reviewed and its importance as an instrument of research had been emphasized, but it had side effects and left impairment of some of the higher mental functions: it also resulted in lasting damage of the frontal lobe areas of the brain. (Dax et al, 1948, 415–26) It is ironic that the approach to curing mental illness recommended by Dax and the establishment he represented, is to sever connections between the patient and parts of the brain; the approach to addressing mental illness represented by psychoanalysis is to reconnect the patient to those parts of the self that have been disconnected and are therefore not functioning to full mature capacity.

Why Wasn't Psychoanalysis Established in Australia?

The short answer is that the Medical Hygiene Authority (MHA) was committed to and quite evangelistic about what they called the new treatments, focusing on the physical body as the locus of mental illness. The Mental Hygiene Authority considered that the new drug regimen and psychosurgery, mostly in the form of leucotomies, were where the cure to mental illness was to be found. Dr John Williams, the honorary psychiatrist to the Royal Children's and Alfred Hospitals in Melbourne sought to discard Freudian theories and in 1952 wrote that he hoped 'many of the existing Freudian doctrines will be numbered among the fantasies of the past.' (Williams, 1952, 29)

Sigmund Freud had challenged prevailing assumptions that mental illness should be treated as a biological dysfunction and began a revolution in how the human mind and madness were to be understood. Freud argued that patients did not need to have their minds rewired through drugs, operations and Electro-convulsive Therapy, nor was it helpful to treat their illness as recalcitrance in need of punishment or deterrence; madness emanates from repression of unwanted feelings, thoughts and desires and Freud proposed that there was a natural tendency in the human psyche towards flight from pain; (Freud, 1895, 307) repression occurs because people instinctively withdraw from painful stimuli. Just as a person takes their hand away from a flame so the psyche tends to withdraw to minimize the immediate distress following psychical trauma. (Breuer & Freud, 1895, 116) For the patient to recover they needed to explore inside of themselves and confront their hidden fears, desires and memories associated with pain. What the asylums did so often was to stop the patient thinking and feeling whilst numbing the pain through drugs and leucotomy in an attempt to drive away the madness.

Freud's argument would suggest that this was flawed at the outset as it wasn't more repression the mad person needed but a confrontation with thoughts and feelings that had been repressed and were erupting out of the person's psyche, but also out of the society in which they exist. But this argument also raises the possibility that the asylum itself participated in this process because it too was structured as a means of repression, and repression lies at the heart of the problem; failure to address this repression ensures the madness continues. The asylums were places of madness in every way.

Aradale actively discouraged psychotherapy and as such discouraged the patients from reflecting or working through their memories, thoughts and feelings which, in the context of psychotherapy would create an environment where the patient could gain some insight into their illness and its genesis and thus lead towards some level of healing.

Pursuing similar arguments, Carl Jung, the founder of analytical psychology understood that what erupts unbidden from the psyche is not limited to contents that have been repressed but also includes content not capable of becoming conscious but which makes its presence known in the form of symptoms. Psychoanalytical thought understands that the dynamics at issue in the formulation of the unconscious are not exhausted by repression but are parts of the psyche that are not developed and as such remain primitive, childlike, reactionary and often erupt unbidden and without moderation.

Analytical psychology would argue that when an individual or group takes any position or direction there is always a part of, an aspect of humanity that is left behind and remains undeveloped and childlike, a part that reacts rather than employing a moderated, thoughtful response.

This is diametrically opposed to the direction taken by Dax and the Mental Hygiene Authority. For Dax it was the bodies of patients that provided observable data for intervention and cure, and it is through the body that invisible and often inarticulate thoughts were easily accessed. Dax engaged patients in art but not to provide a therapeutic environment, nor was his interest in the art of the patient about facilitating expression of emotions or thoughts. His focus was on what the painting could reveal about the patient's illness. Art therapy was not voluntary in the public institutions; patients were sent to art therapy as part of the treatment and the purpose of the painting was to enable the psychiatrists to gather knowledge of the patient so that a diagnosis might be made and a curative effect found and organized into a rational structure, for research, treatment and diagnosis.

Dax employed the commercial artist Edward Adamson on a sessional basis. The purpose of employing Adamson was to secure an artist who did not have any interest in psychoanalysis but who could encourage patients to paint and produce art by offering technical assistance, but not advise on the content, thus not interfering with the validity of the scientific research. And yet the quest for information and research findings gave Dax a great deal of control about interpretation of art and the organisation of a system for its use in hospitals. His project for any diagnostic conclusions from his art began a long-standing research quest for sufficient evidence to prove the content of the art could deepen the psychiatrists understanding of the patient about their clinical condition. By looking at the patient and comparing them with the case notes, he went about formulating a rigorous template of meanings which could be read into art. The translation of emotion into paintings, he argued, might well give valuable information to the psychiatrist, and evidence of a patient's progress might be obtained from their paintings without ever having to discuss them. (Dax, 1949, 238) This antithesis between psychoanalysis and the methods promoted and used by Dax and the MHA, set up and perpetuated a conflict which has endured for decades.

The End of Aradale

Yet for all this process of radical reform, by the 1990s scandal once again continued to emerge regarding the conditions within the asylum system. This time it was to prove fatal to what was no known as Aradale; the unofficial name for the Ararat Mental Hospital. The 1991 Investigative Task Force's Findings on the Aradale Psychiatric Hospital and Residential Institution makes for extremely harrowing reading.

> Intellectually disabled and psychiatrically ill people are amongst the most vulnerable in our community. The majority are unable to speak out or defend their rights. They have to trust the 'system' to do that on their behalf. At Aradale that trust has been broken …

The Task Force repeatedly observed that there are significant numbers of ambulant, apparently high-functioning clients with little to do. This lack of occupation often manifests in sexually inappropriate behaviour, and other behaviours euphemistically called 'challenging' by staff.

These 'challenging behaviours' are used by staff to justify the clients remaining in an institutional environment. The problem is that staff have a vested interest in maintaining clients' dependency. There is a clear perception by staff and the local community that further reduction of existing client numbers will actively threaten employment.

As opposed to a family-like environment, the environment provided to residents and patients is institutionalised. Although the buildings have been maintained and attempts at refurbishment have been made, it is a far cry from 'normal'. Aradale has barely changed since last century.

One of the few changes has been to stop nearly all client participation in daily chores. These 'services' are now performed by a large number of 'non-direct' care staff. The effect of this is to disenfranchise higher functioning clients from participating in or contributing to their own living conditions.

The residents and patients are accommodated in units or wards with about 20 others. Most beds are located in dormitories, there are very few single rooms. There is almost no privacy, even in the ablution facilities. Each unit has a day room and a dining room. Some recreational areas are enclosed by large Cyclone fences. They are barren, uninteresting places, with little in the way of gardens, trees or seating.

It is dependent on which ward the client lives in as to whether he or she will have access to his or her own underwear, or whether the underwear for all the people in the ward is 'pooled'.

A continental breakfast and two hot meals a day are provided. The client cannot choose what he or she eats, although there is a summer menu and a winter menu. There is almost no consistent or meaningful recreational activity provided at Aradale. By and large most clients 'wander' aimlessly around the grounds, or sometimes 'down town'. There is a swimming pool, but that is only open during summer. The golf course, bowling club and tennis court are controlled by private clubs (made up of staff and the public).

There is virtually no provision for meaningful activities during the day. Only 6% of residents have full-time day placements. Yet many residents are quite capable of participating in work, education or recreation on a daily basis. Until the mid-1980s clients (under supervision) used to grow most of the vegetables for the establishment.

Residents and patients provide 74% of their pensions as part-payment for food and board. The balance, approximately $90 per fortnight, is paid into trust. Every fortnight between $20–$80 is withdrawn from their savings in cash by the Charge Nurse. Few residents receive their own money in cash. Most have their money placed in a ward 'pool' for purchasing a wide range of items at the discretion of the staff. Much of this money has been spent on additional items for general consumption, some has been spent on household cleaning agents. Some 'pooled' client funds were spent on basic food items such as milk and fruit to supplement an inadequate diet.

On the occasions a resident or patient goes on holidays or day outings, he or she contributes to all costs (apart from salary) of the accompanying staff, including hotel bills, drinks and meals. On these trips staff keep all client monies in cash and dole it out to residents or patients or spend it how they see fit. Staff can rarely account properly for how

> the clients' money is spent. The residents' medical care is provided by local general practitioners at cost to Medicare. The residents do not get access to psychologists, social workers or occupational therapists. Some specialist medical services are paid for directly by residents at above the scheduled fee. No resident has private health insurance and the shortfall between the specialist fee charged and the Medicare rebate, if any, is paid out of the resident's savings. Dental care is seriously deficient. Many patients and residents are without either their own teeth or false teeth. Aradale does not supply money for dentures. Many of the shortcomings in daily care, programs, sustenance and shelter were blamed on a lack of resources. The Task Force completely rejects this…
>
> Stock control is non-existent. Accumulation of stock in many areas make thefts difficult to detect and, if detected, it is virtually impossible for the police to gain sufficient evidence to effectively prosecute.

The Task Force found that 20–50% of some items of food purchased by Aradale did not reach the clients' plates. The extensive discussion of cost efficiency and financial management in this report is not based on economic rationalist ideals. There are two compelling issues arising from the Task Force's findings:

> i) Aradale has lost focus on what its primary function should be. Resources have been utilised not only without regard to improving conditions but at a direct cost to client independence; and
> Resources for clients,
> ii) Wasted resources at Aradale must be redirected to maintaining clients in community settings with improved community support services.
>
> (VPARL 1988–92)

Further to this, the report discussed a wide variety of appalling cases of sexual assault, prostitution and abuse which, while found to be unsupported, featured rebuttals to such claims on apparently feeble seeming evidence such as,

> a) the issue of consent was confused, given the woman was allegedly asking for cigarettes as payment for intercourse;
>
> b) the matter was not reported to the police at the time;

Collectively the weight of this report and its horrific findings regarding conditions within Aradale led to the closure of the hospital as part of a broader controversial move towards deinstitutionalization of the mental health system. The public release of the report and the humiliation it represented for its staff as well as the detrimental effects upon Ararat's employment, is still a point of contention and some anger today. This lies at the heart of continuing conflicts over the management and use of the site in heritage and tourism.

> MELBOURNE: The Victorian Government has announced it will close the controversial Aradale Training Centre for the intellectually disabled by 1994. The former asylum, at Ararat in central-western Victoria, was the subject of a damning Health Department inquiry late last year which documented abuse of patients. The Commonwealth Human Rights Commissioner, Brian Burdekin, demanded at one time that Aradale be bulldozed.
>
> Announcing the closure, the Minister for Community Services, Kay Setches, said even a massive injection of funding would not make the centre a fit place to live in.
>
> She said the Health Department had documented shocking and inadequate conditions where residents slept 30 to a dormitory and 'had no real dignity and no real privacy'.

'They were bored. They were locked up and they shared clothing,' she said. 'Their opportunity to develop to their full given potential has been cruelly cut off years ago.' Ms Setches said about 100 of the current 186 residents would be relocated to community units in Ararat, Stawell and other towns in the immediate region. Staff from Aradale would work with the intellectually disabled in the units.

All but 16 of the remaining residents would be relocated in supported community houses or more appropriate care facilities. The majority of the 280 staff from Aradale would continue working in the region. A small number would move to other parts of the state to accompany residents. Some staff would be offered transfers, retraining or voluntary redundancy.

The Health Department's forensic unit for psychiatric patients on the Aradale site will remain open.

The closure is part of a long-term plan to, where possible, move intellectually disabled people into community support houses by the year 2000. Yesterday's announcement was followed by the release of the ALP election policy on services for people with intellectual disabilities, the first policy released by Labor ahead of the election, which is due before the end of the year. (*Canberra Times*, 20.7.1992, 16)

Dax's Legacy and 1992 Commission and Deinstitutionalisation

Cunningham Dax carefully cultivated himself as the image of a hero, a knight errant and saviour of the Dickensian Aradale psychiatric hospital and dilapidated mental health system that had endured even through the post war years. In the mythology of the knight errant hero, the Holy Grail is not only difficult to find and even more difficult to obtain, it is also illusory. In the Arthurian legends Arthur never finds the Holy Grail but

Sir Galahad does because of the purity of his heart. The Holy Grail is the legendary cup that Jesus used at the last supper and as such it is attached to the idea of suffering, healing and resurrection. (Tether, 2017) Dax thought he could find a way to cure mental illness, that it would be a thing of the past through the scientific administration of drugs, electro-convulsive therapy and leucotomy. Dax's focus on pathologizing mental illness and finding a cure through medical intervention prevented him from accessing other resources that would have been profoundly important in his quest to properly address mental illness. For him it was a biologically generated malady.

Some of his approaches have echoes of current therapeutic methodology, for instance, he encouraged and participated in the practice of what he called art therapy, but it was not art therapy as it is practiced today. Dax's use of patients' art seems to be part of a continuum of the way in which he viewed and used chemical treatments and psychosurgery. The patient was encouraged to express what came to mind, but not as a therapy for the patient so much as a means of the psychiatrist gaining insight into the symptoms and so further developing an understanding of the medical treatment used and required. Dax wanted the patients to be in a state of calm, but his work also was intentionally designed to smother and disguise the pre-existent illness. This created difficulties in treating those who had received a number of different medications, where it was harder to identify which drug had which effect when so many had been taken in at different times in a person's life. (Dax, 1992, 99) There was little attempt to investigate any social or personality-based factors which may have lain behind a patients illness, nor any attempt to work with a patient to understand their condition or find internal resources to re-orientate their thinking and responses. Dax actively discouraged psychotherapy. The power of cure lay in the practitioner, not in the patient.

The optimism towards this biological treatment in the 1940s and 1950s was reflected in a widespread increase in confidence that there would be a cure for mental illness. Dax encouraged the asylums to practice openness and encouraged family and community to assist mental health professionals by implementing community networks. This direction created challenges to the authority of psychiatry as the families of patients, their wider networks and other professionals in the health departments sought to influence the structures by which mental health services were administered and delivered. Dax sought to encourage the movement of patients from the asylums and back into the families and communities from which they had come. Care was in the process of becoming community rather than institutionally based. This move was intended to enlarge the scope of the profession but paradoxically introduced an element of competition in determining the dominant paradigm for understanding and treating mental illness. Dax's era of enlightened leadership and benevolent autocracy was undermined by the prescription of the service delivery framework.

The Dax Art Collection is an extensive compilation of his patients creations gathered during his years as Superintendent of Netherne Hospital in Surrey and later as Chair of the Mental Hygiene Authority in Victoria, Australia. The Dax collection has preserved in image of psychiatry's golden age; the collection represents a period before his approaches came under the scrutiny and criticism that ensued in the1960's and 1970's. The initial focus of the scrutiny was the treatment which accompanied his art therapy, that is, ECTs and leucotomies and the unfounded optimism of the curability of mental illness.

The New Directions Policy of 1986 reinvented the administrative structures and decentralised mental health services through regionalisation. This policy proposed integration of all health services and placed the consumer as the central focus of the network of services. (Bircanon and Plenty, 1986, 58–61) However, for an individual living with a mental illness, learning to live in a community setting posed challenges that were often difficult to overcome. Quite apart from the issue of institutionalisation that accompanied incarceration in an asylum, Community Mental Health agencies were required to respond to everyone's specific needs, thus requiring a shift on how services were delivered and how mental health workers needed to be trained.

State run psychiatric hospitals had traditionally been the primary component in the treatment of people with mental illness. For many years, diagnosis described individuals with behavioural or emotional disorders which substantially interfered with or limited their life activities or impacted negatively on the lives of those around them. As such, these people were kept out of the community and institutionalised. But even the institutional setting is not without its difficulties; a primary difficulty is the absence of hope for the patient and their families, and the expectation that the patient would probably never recover. (Patrick, 2007, 18–188) There was also the ever-present problem of asylums being misused as a means of removing people who were an impediment to others. The case of Dr Carr described in Chapter One, illustrates this phenomena. In short institutions seemed to become warehouses where the mentally ill or those deemed such for whatever reason, were kept for long periods of time with little expectation of improvement or release.

The benefits of the proposed deinstitutionalization were that the individuals would obtain a better quality of life and more independence outside of the institution; this would lead to a reduction in the need for psychotropic medication and create increased socialization and adaptability to change. In practice, this was not always realized. The individuals who were to receive these benefits of deinstitutionalization were often inadequately supported, frequently homeless, isolated and often victimized. Many who were released from institutionalization deteriorated and were repeatedly admitted and then released from hospitalization.

Fear of people with mental illness is still common, and alienation, abuse and poor hygiene and health are often added to the mental difficulties. The mentally ill are frequently victims of rejection, stigmatization and harassment and so become unsupported and at high risk of self-harm. For many people with mental illness, they traded the isolation of the institution for isolation within community.

Cunningham Dax opened up the asylums. They were no longer places where the doings behind the walls were secrets held by the staff and unspoken by the patients for fear of reprisal, incarceration or abuse. The world knew what was occurring and the actions of the system were open to scrutiny. He also attempted to work from a theoretical and evidence-based model to assess what affect treatments had upon the patients and demanded of his departments that meticulous records were kept. He involved the communities in the care of the mentally ill, so taking them, by stages, out of the cells and into the society. But at the same time, his criterion for improvement lay in the concept of manageability, not creativity. The power was placed firmly in the hands of the professionals resulting in a perpetuated disempowering of the patients. There was no acknowledgement that the patients had power within themselves to contribute to their own cure or to be a part of their own cure. They were recipients of prescribed treatment. There was also no perception that mental illness may have been indicative of adopted structures of coping that, with good guidance and skilled exploration, may have resulted in the mentally ill learning new skills and means of adapting that would not only bring healing but strengthen and enhance the patients' former capacity to contribute to their world and thrive. His legacy set up a conflict of interest between biologically based psychiatry and talking therapies which has endured to the present.

Front View of the Lunatic Asylum (Ararat), 1880.
http://handle.slv.vic.gov.au/10381/151015

Back View of the Lunatic Asylum (Ararat), 1880.
http://handle.slv.vic.gov.au/10381/151017

Ararat Asylum Tours, 2015.
Courtesy Eerie Tours

Ghost Tour Ararat Asylum, 2017.
Courtesy Eerie Tours

Opening of the Railway to Ararat: views of the town and district, 1875. Hugh George for Wilson and MacKinnon, Melbourne.
http://handle.slv.vic.gov.au/10381/103242

'Sacking' a wife at Cape Schanck, 1877. Richard Egan Lee, Melbourne.
http://handle.slv.vic.gov.au/10381/172501

Ararat Asylum, 1869. Harrison, W. H & Cooke, A. C. (Albert Charles), 1836–1902 (artist). Ebenezer and David Syme, Melbourne.
http://handle.slv.vic.gov.au/10381/151373

Caricature of Dr Thomas Embling as a naïve idealist. In addition to his work at the Yarra Bend Asylum he is known for supporting political reform, the rebellion at Eureka and assisted the introduction of Llamas and camels into Australia. Image taken from *Mr Embling in Arcadia,* 1856. Printed and published by Edgar Ray and Frederick Sinnett, Melbourne

6

Ghosts of the Past

What Does it Mean to Be Haunted?

> What is a ghost? A tragedy condemned to repeat itself time and time again? An instant of pain perhaps. Something dead which still seems to be alive. An emotion suspended in time like a blurred photograph, like an insect trapped in amber. (Del Toro, *The Devils Backbone*, https://www.imdb.com/title/tt0256009/)

From ancient times, in folk tales of cultures around the world there have been ghost stories, that is, tales of spirits who return from the dead to haunt the places they left behind. In ancient Mesopotamia death was never passive; it was the final act of life. The underworld was where the souls of the dead ate dirt and supped from mud puddles. It was the place from which there was no return unless by special dispensation from Erishkigal, the Queen of the underworld. Dispensation to leave might be granted to right a wrong encountered during mortal lifetime. (Thokild, 1975) Australian Aboriginals have ghost stories, but they are normally associated with the dreamtime and associated storytelling: a means of passing on the wisdom of the moiety. (Clarke, 2007) Ghost stories are encountered in all of the

African nations, usually connected to horror of some kind, and in our own western culture ghosts are usually a signifier of some past evil, a tormented soul unable to find rest because a great wrong of their lifetime has not been resolved. The similarities as much as the diversities of these understandings around the content of the word ghost, begs the question 'What is a ghost?' Is a ghost a reminder of a trauma, a moment of searing pain, a suspended emotion, a creature moribund, or is it an insect caught in amber, a moment in time preserved in perfect stasis? (Triggs, 2016) Ghost images distort the boundaries of time between past and present; the trapped insect belongs to the past but has nevertheless been preserved into the present as something that has resisted decay and erosion, preserved like an IVF embryo waiting to be implanted and as such has outlived its own death but not found transition from it.

Ghosts are like clues from a detective story; there has been an incident and the ghost and the observer of the ghost participate in a dance macabre that alludes to the event but only obliquely, something seen out of the corner of the mind, in the periphery of vision, carrying both the potential to elucidate the origin or to be simply seen and not comprehended as anything more than an encounter. However, if the encounter is explored, comprehended and addressed, possibly the ghost may be laid to rest. If not, the trauma must endure and recur, if not in the mind of the person encountering the ghost perhaps in another who also, in some way, enters into the drama. In this sense, the ghost cannot exist except through the one who does the encountering, the one who in some way is immersed, even if for a moment, in the initial drama. Ghosts are an archetypal experience common to all cultures and times, classes and generations. Carl Jung proposed that archetypes are unconscious universal structures, inherited blueprints or templates by which the human mind organizes and forms its energy along repeatable and recognizable pathways. These innate patterns or predispositions manifest themselves through images, symbols, myths and folklores which bear the commonality of the human psyche and the divergence of individual cultures.

The British Exeter University scholar and folklorist, Theodora Brown, suggests that although ghosts appear to be autonomous to us and unbidden, they are all about us; they come from within us, a projection from our internal world. Brown posits that the landscape determines the ghosts that make themselves known. (Brown, 1982) In 2014, retired policeman Harry Martindale claimed that when he was a young man he saw around twenty Roman soldiers, visible only from the knees up, marching through the cellar of the Treasurer's House in York. (*York Press*, 16.10.2014) Some years later, excavations revealed that the old Roman road into the garrison at York (Eboracum) used to run through where the Treasurer's House was later built, and was about fifteen inches lower than the cellar floor. York lends itself to ghostly encounters; it reeks of layers of history; it engages the senses through multiple mediums, our sense of the history, the architecture, the layers we know exist, the smells, the accent of the Yorkies, the stories being constantly told, and the knowledge that the 9th Legion disappeared after heading north from York. There is no way of objectively verifying a sighting of a ghostly legion but it is clear that the architecture and culture of York lends itself to encounters with shadows of the past.

This absorption of the geography presented in old historic cities like York with its dark winding and narrow streets accentuates a survival mechanism within us; it brings to the surface processes from our ancient past that have evolved over time to protect us from harm, from enemies, from predators. If you are walking through a dark and narrow street or wooded area and hear the sound of footsteps or rustling in the night-time, your response will be an increased or heightened level of arousal and attention. What I mean by this is you would act 'as if' there was a wilful agent around, about to do you harm. We have evolved to err on the side of perceiving threats in ambiguous situations and these perceived threats activate hypervigilance, for malevolent supernatural or natural agents abound in the dark, especially where the architecture of alleyways, houses and buildings have unpleasant smells, rattling or creaking sounds, where the wind creates sighing or howling as it passes through cracks and openings and where we find echoes and cold spots.

What does it mean for a place to be perceived as a haunted site? What even is a ghost in this context? And what is the popular perception of ghosts and the notion of site in any given particular culture or time? Aradale is perceived to be a 'haunted' site. People pay well to go on ghost tours of the site and others pay more to go on ghost hunting expeditions, almost always at night. Ghost stories and hauntings attached to places like Aradale contain social anxieties and phobias from the past. Ghosts may serve as a convenient metaphor for a whole host of matters that we are uneasy about, many not associated with the supernatural but ghosts provide a means of articulating those problems, a means of processing and making sense of experiences that might overwhelm or mystify. Aradale's history is of unimaginable suffering for those incarcerated in its environment and partly because of our knowledge of this suffering, madness or being designated mad is a fearful thing, even today; these dark spaces in our minds are assumed to hide within Aradale's darkest recesses and forgotten margins. The place threatens with all the fears and imaginations of those who have tried to stake out spaces to protect their health and happiness, and those from whom these spaces were unequivocally stripped. It was the fear of our dark spaces and forgotten margins that gave rise to a movement in the modern era advocating for the opening up of the dark and unspoken to light and air, and this led to the construction of designated places of containment for disease: hospitals and asylums. British society, proud of its technological and scientific achievements, believed it could openly face all things. There was no need for superstition or fear in this age of enlightenment and reason, so that which had been feared could now be contained and dealt with. These designated spaces were meant to keep society free from perceived ills and dangers and they were also designed to be therapeutic. But the moment a space is created to separate out that which is threatening, a space is created in which the threat is contained, a place without space and without light. Aradale is constructed on a hillside, separate from but overlooking the town. It is surrounded by walls, hidden but functional. The unacknowledged fear that was still existent in the collective mind and generated the creation of the asylums, remained a dark force in their function and sustenance. In essence, as humans seek to extract, regulate and separate the self from the object of fear and phobia, space is shaped, structured and transformed by another external force; space becomes haunted as humans extract and imbed their fears and phobias, betraying the reality of suffering and anxiety within.

In this light, ghosts, while often a subject for ridicule by sceptics, fulfil important functions that reflect and expose social anxieties, manifested in uncanny experiences of the supernatural. In 'The Uncanny', Freud discusses the means by which the psyche achieves disentanglement of the conscious from the unconscious, the modern from the primal. (Freud, 1990, 339–76) While his focus is primarily on the function of the psyche, his work also pertains to fundamental existential questions regarding one's sense of being in the world. He describes the uncanny through the use of the oppositional terms 'heimlich' and 'unheimlich'; heimlich referring to the sense of the comforting and familiar and, in contrast, unheimlich referring to the strange and inaccessible. Ernst Jentch proposes that the uncanny is linked to intellectual uncertainty about the status of an object, animated or inanimate, alive or dead. Unheimlich is that which should have remained a secret or hidden but which has come to light. In short, the word suggests that a lack of orientation is bound up with the impression of the uncanniness of a thing or an incident. (Jentsch, 1906, 352) For Freud, uncanny experiences occur when the comforting and familiar become entangled with the strange, rendering them both familiar and alienated. In this experience there occurs a duality in which one has a sense of being in and out of place at the same time. In an experience of haunting, this dichotomy characterises precisely the moment when repressed tensions and anxieties of the past return to haunt the present. (Freud, 1990, 340) By themselves, psychological approaches to the uncanny can fail to do justice to the rich complexities surrounding both experiences of haunting and the perpetuating of ghost stories in local folklore. As Bath and Newton argue in their research into popular beliefs on haunting and the supernatural in seventeenth-century England, functionalist perspectives have a tendency to write out the complexities of existing eschatological beliefs and the complex web of symbolism in which people both share stories and have phenomenological experiences of the supernatural. There is a paradox in this; hauntings are often linked to terror and terror produces a dis-ease. So why do some individuals take delight in terrifying themselves through horror movies, horror literature, ghost stories, embarking on ghost tours and searching for ghostly encounters? These endeavours are prominent in modern culture and support a thriving commercial industry. It is worth taking a moment to reflect on the varied nuances of horror and terror. Terror from the Latin *terrorum* means extreme fear while horror from the modern Latin verb *horrere* means to stand up, to bristle or to shudder, which could be defined as the shuddering of intensity; the person is hypervigilant and ready for action. Thus, while terror refers to the mental state associated with fear, horror refers more to the physical response to that which is not as it should be; horror has semantic overtones of disgust and repugnance. (Connolly, 2003)

Terror is immensely personal and associated with an ultimate threat, the threat of non-being. Horror is more attuned to the function of the observer or hearer, Terror is immediate and engages primitive responses of survival whereas horror engages the developed, rational brain, instigating value judgements and moral reflection. With horror, one can think that what is happening is awful, shocking, wrong. With terror, it is not about thinking; it is about surviving and feeling. There is a thrill in horror but a thrill that is nevertheless about an observed encounter and while one may be, as an onlooker, deeply involved in an emotive response, there is not the sense of terror that accompanies, for instance, an encounter with a predator in which the observer is on the menu and may quite possibly be destroyed. With horror there is a sense that one may have the thrill but still not have one's existence truly threatened.

This is the underlying context behind the very successful business of ghost tours and haunting experiences associated with Ararat Lunatic Asylum. Ghost stories and the haunting experience are primarily focused on the notion of trauma. They bind communities together through the act and ritual of story-telling and the rituals and symbols of the haunting experiences. They also, even if the story is not precisely true, refer to sites of horror, anxiety and social tension through their symbolic representation in folklore. They are given emotional poignancy in the act of retelling the experience or tale and work to symbolically connect the people of the present with traumatic experiences of the past. There are parallels here, in this respect, between 'dark tourism' and the ghost tour industry at Aradale and those at other sites such as Port Arthur or even Auschwitz. As Gordon argues, the ghost and the haunted experience are multi-layered symbols that refer to loss, trauma and injustice. (Gordon, 2008) They refer to powerful taboos surrounding death, fear, insanity, torment and sexuality that are fundamentally uncanny and blur the boundaries of reason and human experience. In a sense, the 'haunting effect' and the terror of ghosts draws attention to these sites of trauma and undermines our attempts to rationalize them away through the overwhelming and unsettling nature of the uncanny experiences they engender.

As Owens argues, ghosts closely mirror our times. They reflect the culture, the preoccupations, the moods and anxieties of their age. They are not always the insubstantial shapes and apparitions we tend to think of. A contemporary haunting experience might be manifested in a fleeting sense of a cold touch on the shoulder, a shape drifting towards a door or faint images appearing in a photograph; a medieval ghost might be 'more likely to break down the door and beat you to death with the broken planks.' (Owens, 2017, 9) Medieval stories of ghosts were often indistinguishable from other more mundane encounters; they were part of a culture of strange tell-tale signs of the supernatural in the wildlife, temperature fluctuations which alerted people to another presence, marks left on frames and lintels to keep evil spirits away and objects and marks left behind in their wake when they did come by, manifested often in some hideous injury or anachronistic clothing.

> While writers associated with the 'graveyard school' in the mid-eighteenth century invited us down into the crypt and conjured up macabre spectres to remind us of our mortality,

> the romantics saw the world differently; for them, ghosts could tell us about the most secret corners of our souls. And from the 1890s until the Second World War, artists and writers took ghosts out of the historic mansions and urban homes they had so vigorously haunted for most of the Victorian era and re-located them in the heart of the country, down leafy lanes, deep within ancient barrows and along the routes of old pilgrim paths. (Owens, 2017, 9)

Ghostly encounters in the twenty first century seem to have moved from the environment in which people live their day to day existence. They have become a recreational consumerable which people travel to haunted sites to encounter, in a place where that which was once commonplace may be found again, in a place where haunting may be assured.

There are many well-established ghost stories associated with the Ararat Asylum and these have been recorded in local papers and in social media commentary by tourists. One of the examples cited were claims the Administration Building was haunted by the ghost of Dr Mullen, the superintendent who suicided with cyanide in his office in 1912, despite his having actually died in his home. (*Border Morning Mail and Riverina Times*, 21.8.1912, 3) Another was that in the women's ward, staff would see a woman in nineteenth century costume on level two accompanied by the sound of high heeled steps. Some customers on ghost tours had taken blurry pictures of a distant figure and posted these on social media. There were stories of people claiming to be scratched while in the women's hospital; some women claimed they felt as if they were pregnant. People reported seeing a ghostly figure on the steps of the main hall and others, a man on the stair-well, despite the stairs having long since rotted and collapsed. In the cellar, people on tour claimed to suffer from inexplicable blood noses and it is a common site of panic and hyperventilation. There are also claims that the strong scent of formaldehyde permeates the hospital building and mortuary. In the men's ward, women on tour claimed to be choked, punched and sexually assaulted by unseen hands, leading to some tourists 'losing their shit' and needing to be removed from the tour. There is a claim that people hear running and see ghostly figures on the site. Windows in the men's ward are reputed to show faces which promptly disappear with echoed screams heard late at night.

Alongside these narratives were stories of a different nature, stories of mistaken identity where living people had been taken for ghosts and scepticism that provided reasoned causes for what others assumed were supernatural encounters. Given the site has also been used as temporary ad-hoc shelter for local homeless people it is hardly surprising that strange noises and figures are sometimes seen late at night. On one occasion former staff told the story of several ghost tour operators closing the site after seeing a pale woman with no shoes and a white dress slowly making her way across the courtyard at a staggered gate. They called out to her to no avail and began to feel uneasy as they approached her nervously and increasingly 'wigged out'. Upon reaching the woman the remaining tour guide, who had plucked up enough courage to speak to her, realized she was a straggler from a tour and was 'absolutely wasted' and looking for one of her shoes that had fallen off on tour. He reflected that if he had lacked the courage to approach her, he would have been utterly convinced he had seen a ghost that night. Some claim to have encountered famous and infamous patients of the past, such as the story that the ghost of self-mutilator Gary Webb screamed at visitors to 'Get out!' of his room. Another claim was that the Superintendent's office was haunted and visitors experienced a bitter taste while walking by. Despite the fact as, as previously mentioned, he died in his own home. (https://www.mamamia.com.au/ararat-mental-asylum-australias-haunted-building/) Some people claimed to have fallen into trances, others reported hearing screams and being shoved and bitten. (https://realparanormalexperiences.com/ararat-lunatic-asylum-the-haunting) Perhaps key to all these stories is that there is a perceived link, that haunting experiences are manifestations of the horrors and traumas of the past. As argued in the *Herald Sun*.

> Perhaps rumours of the supernatural are true. If such ghastly occurrences were to exist, surely it would be the result of 130 years of mass physical and mental abuse. Surely such atrocities would scar the very souls of victims and push them to wander the empty halls of the Ararat Lunatic Asylum – unable to escape even after death. Alternatively, the speculations of beings from the afterlife haunting this facility could ruminate from the imagination of local tour guides, keen to cash in on the undeniable curiosity the supernatural evokes. Either way the history of Ararat, disturbing as it may be, is worth considering. Only then can we understand just how tough the mentally ill of history had it and hope that such mistakes are never repeated. (https://www.heraldsun.com.au/news/victoria/victorian-psychiatric-patients-grim-fate-in-hellish-1800s-hospitals/news-story/c7928ebe8a9f527a941cce86e0990fef)

The proliferation of these experiences raises some interesting questions. Is it really possible for traumatic experiences to leave these emotional and psychical scars on the landscape and in the walls of these historic buildings the way these perceived haunting experiences seem to suggest? By what mechanisms can sites like the Ararat Mental Hospital, marred by a traumatic and tumultuous history, induce these experiences even though significant changes in space, time and locality have occurred? Is this more a product of cultural cues rooted deeply in psychological archetypes enmeshed in webs of folklore and popular culture?

At base is a notion that haunted locations are what Basso refers to as 'topographies of remembrance' that reflect, via the experience of haunting, patterns of unique features of distinct cultural and historical contexts. It is proposed that many hauntings are social, fragments of individual (or group) practices of remembering. This is not always a symbolic 'ghosts of place'. This remembering, as the essence of a social haunting, is both synchronic and diachronic. The idea of a haunting as synchronic means that it has a meaning, right here and now for the person experiencing the haunting. Synchronic comes from the Greek terms *sun* – meaning 'with', and *chronos* – time. The haunting is encountered in place as a manifestation of past practices but it is interpreted in the moment of the ghostly encounter in the present, with all of the presuppositions, understandings and interpretations of the present. But as this synchronic bundle of acts (and/or habits), it manifests diachronically through time (*dia* – through, *chronos* – time). The haunting is evocative of a history, a process, an evolution that is what it is because it has passed through a chronological process. In a similar vein, the experience of haunting is also diachronic. It happens within a history, a process that carries with it the accrued expectations of centuries of folklore, cultural shifts and appropriations from diverse cultural streams. In this sense, hauntings are dynamic in that they emerge out of the mnemonic environment in which they are encountered.

Hauntings are usually perceived negatively, that is associated with a trauma, sometimes even demonically, perhaps because positive hauntings achieve less notoriety. Hauntings may be attendant to a unique emotional experience, perhaps some physical characteristic of a place, custom/tradition, social event, ritual, or a 'rite of passage' that no longer exists, and are frequently associated with a person's cultural heritage, a more intimate and productive 'other' means of interaction with place. Such hauntings are often representative of unique and memorable places of specific significance. (Basso, 1996)

Commercialization of the Ghost Story

What stands in stark contrast between the ghost of folklore and that of contemporary haunted locations is that the contemporary 'haunted' heritage sites are frequently commodified as sites of dark tourism. These sites live in a constant process of change driven by a symbiotic relationship between popular culture, folklore, social memory and the demands of tourism. The commodification of hauntings is not new. Julian Holloway discusses how chroniclers in 1762 noted that the story of the infamous

Cock Lane ghost story of London's Smithfield helped 'all the taverns and alehouses in the neighbourhood [to] make fortunes' and he relates how eighteenth and nineteenth century fascination with the supernatural led to a thriving ghost tourism industry in remote parts of Scotland, Ireland and Wales. (Halloway, 2010) However, in the late twentieth and early twenty-first centuries this romanticist underbelly of enlightenment recasting of the supernatural as a curiosity to be experienced, has become remodelled through the transformative effect of mass media and marketing. Davies argues that there has been a reversal of the historic position where communities desired to be rid of their spirits and were duty-bound to 'lay the ghost'. In our present context, 'the ghost is a desirable lodger rather than an unwelcome guest'. (Davies, 2007, 64)

In concert with the broader framework of popular culture and commodification, Ghost-tours draw on traditional aspects of storytelling as an art form. Rhythm, delivery and narrative are tied to social consequence as integral parts of the experience. As Halloway comments,

> The performative force of legend-telling is achieved through style, content, and pacing. Furthermore, these are dialogical events where teller and listener are produced and drawn into relation and where aesthetic expectations in the audience, derived through inter-semiotic and intertextual translation, are drawn upon and sustained. The tale is thus not the product of one single stage of performance but of multiple and resonating (mediated) sites in which `cultural memories are played out, thereby shaping meaning-making processes at play within these walks'
>
> Participants, as they wander between the stops, discuss horror films or supernatural novels they have read and watched, emphasising the mediated legend and its telling. Often audience expectations remain implicit though on some tours, in expressing disappointment with the walks, tourists reveal the expectation of entertainment value. Indeed, tour

> guides can be explicit about how they draw upon audience expectations and how they reproduce generic ghost-storytelling markers: discussing the exuberant and knowing exaggeration of his storytelling style, one guide remarked to me, 'Well everybody loves a bit of hammyness don't they?' (Holloway, 2010)

Ghost tours have become an international phenomenon since the late 20th century with versions of the walking ghost tour held in most cities across Europe, the Americas, Asia and Australasia. In many cases competing tours are run over the same location by rival companies. In Ararat there are the Lantern Tours at the site of J Ward, situated at the former Ararat Prison converted to house the criminally insane during the 1890s, and Eerie Tours which conduct walking tours and ghost hunting tours at Aradale as well as Ballarat and the Ballarat Old Cemetery. Eerie Tours also offer paranormal investigation tours where patrons utilise group vigils, Ouija boards, séances, and different technologies (such as meters that measure electromagnetic frequencies) in the presence of claimed mediums and psychics. All of this represents a fundamental transformation of the role of ghosts and hauntings through the broader process of technologization of the haunting experience and participates in a process which Holloway describes as representative of '...The binary approach, in which ghosts, the occult, and magic do not disappear completely but are marginalized in various ways as residual phenomena both subordinate to and explicable by modernity's rational and secular tenets.' (Halloway, 2010, 4) This argument is only the tip of a more complicated process whereby supernaturalism, far from being monolithic, is constructed of diverse cultural frameworks, structures and epistemologies which exist in multiple and contradictory relations to one another. (Halloway, 2010) As McEwan comments,

> Enchantment can be a state in which ghosts, spirits, and spectres exist within a melange of other marvels, including magic, myth, monsters, witchcraft, sorcery, voodoo,

> vampires, and zombies ... Such marvels are no longer thought to have been exorcised by the rational and secular processes of modernity; far from being extraneous to modernity, they are intrinsic to what are increasingly recognised as thoroughly enchanted modernities. (McEwen, 2008)

This commodified engagement with ghosts is perhaps a truly westernised representation of the connection between supernatural belief and scientific rationalization whereby the folkloric and supernatural nature of ghosts has become transformed by technology and mass media into a curiosity to be experienced and mediated through capitalism, technological apparatus and popular culture. There is another level of complexity at work here where a deeply troubling history, tied to significant issues of social justice, is part of a process of conceptualization within the community between diverse stake holders with different interests in the site. Yet the site is also in a continual process of framing and reframing critical social issues through the primal impact of folkloric archetypes, changing perceptions of mental illness, the impact of popular culture and the process of commodification.

7

The Ghost Wars

Battles for Control of the Past

> Over almost 130 years, the lunatic asylum housed thousands of patients ranging from the criminally insane to those who suffered from mental illness and other conditions. Aradale Mental Hospital saw many deaths in its walls, and after an Ararat ghost tour, you'll see that some of these patients never really escaped their imprisonment in these hallowed walls.
>
> Aradale Ghost Tour is one of the creepiest ghost tours in Australia. Prepare to be haunted by stories of bizarre history, brutal treatments, amazing personal stories, and of course, lots of ghost stories detailing some of the most infamous people to walk these halls. (https://www.eerietours.com.au/tours/aradale-ghost-tour/)

The 15 years following the closure of the asylum were not kind to Aradale. When the last patient was rehoused the government was left with a glaring issue: What is to be done with a massive, purpose-built rural lunatic asylum?

This is a question which has challenged governments around the world, particularly those in the United Kingdom and United States where large numbers of enormous edifices with accommodation for sometimes thousands of patients now sit without purpose. A small percentage located in more urban regions have been redeveloped, but many were subjected to the slow fate of demolition by neglect, their only purpose to provide graffiti-covered environments for urban explorers on YouTube.

It seems significant that what was created as a state-of-the-art construct with beautiful surrounding gardens, was left to rot and decay, firstly in its ethos and practice and now in its physical reality. The beautifully designed surrounding gardens, intended to offer the patients a safe and therapeutic environment, now express physically the neglect and decay of the functioning asylum. It seems significant that the intention, having been subverted and degraded throughout its history, was the only reality that could be conceived. That having failed, the space could not be reimagined; the very structure was so integrated with the function that when the function failed, so did the entire edifice. The buildings and gardens have not been pulled down or transformed into something other; they have been left to decay and deteriorate into ruins.

The psychiatric institution of Aradale was a self-contained entity within the Ararat area. Until it closed, Aradale had been the largest employer in the region. That it is left to decay is symbolic of the space its history occupies in the collective psyche of Ararat. In some senses Aradale is still a major employer for Ararat but now through tourist and hospitality industries, specifically because it is a 'ghostly' place and that identity alone brings trade to shops, restaurants and hotels in Ararat. Aradale is symbolic for the people of Ararat; it represents something else, something indefinable yet very much part of the collective memory. Jung conjectures that the language of all human beings is full of symbols (Jung, 1964, 3) and proposes that symbols are language or images that convey, by means of concrete reality, something hidden or unknown. They have a numinous quality only dimly perceived by the conscious mind. These symbols can never be fully understood by the conscious mind. In symbols, the opposites are united in a form that is 'never devised consciously, but always produced out of the unconscious by way of revelation or intuition.'

(Jung, 1964, 48) In this sense, the symbol is integrative in that it is a union of opposites, holding in tension the different aspects of the psyche. And it is also compensatory in that it illuminates something that belongs to the domain of the unconscious. It compensates for that which is hidden from our conscious mind. I am suggesting that there is still much hidden in the collective mind of Ararat, and the malaise regarding the use of the building will not be resolved until the hidden and unconscious has been known and integrated into the collective psyche. Of all the ideas proposed for the use of Aradale, there have always been stumbling blocks that have rendered solutions impracticable.

The Victorian Government had grand plans for Aradale after its closure. Ararat sits in the middle of wine country and local producers have manufactured shiraz for over a hundred and fifty years. The authorities decided to capitalise on this and leased the site to a Melbourne based tertiary institution, Northern Melbourne Institute of TAFE. The intention of the TAFE (Technical and Further Education) was to use the hectares around Aradale as a vineyard for students who would find accommodation in the asylum during their training, but the course failed, maybe due to the already growing reputation of the asylum and maybe because of inadequate funding and demand.

The vineyard continued to produce with minimal staff and once again the historic sections of Aradale stood desolate without use, the only regular visitor being the security guard vainly attempting to keep vandals from smashing windows. Decay began to spread. Paint peeled. Spiders created webs. Dust gathered on windowsills. Possums and bats nested in attics. Day by day, Aradale became less useable, its decay only adding to its ominous façade in the minds of the few adventurers who were able to sneak over the fence.

The summer of 2011 was to prove significant in the story of Aradale when the front doors of Aradale were first opened for customers eager to explore the asylum in what was to become a highly successful ghost tour business.

Three years prior, Nathaniel Buchanan, a tour guide new to the region, had been invited to a photoshoot being held at Aradale over a weekend. Nathaniel had graduated from the University of Queensland with an honours degree in history and qualification to teach. Finding classroom life dull, he secured a position as a tour guide for Contiki Europe which saw him talking to people not just about the glamour of Paris and Vienna but also some of its dark locations and attractions such as battlefields, catacombs, concentration camps, and Dracula's Castle, all on the itineraries.

Nathaniel was fascinated with the history of these locations and his position gave him an insight into how the general public reacts to such stories when confronted with the actual locations themselves. Reactions differed but tears, silence and melancholia were fairly consistent. When done respectfully, the tour guide was always deeply thanked for taking the visitors on such an emotional journey. Nathaniel began enjoying the reaction and when his time with Contiki ended he specialised his guiding skills by gaining employment in, and studying, some of the more popular ghost tours in the United Kingdom such as London, York and Edinburgh.

Returning to Australia, he lived onsite as a presenter in the Port Arthur Ghost Tour, a site famous for the brutality and mortality of the convict settlement there, and here he familiarised himself with the idiosyncrasies of Australian Dark Tourism. With this background he visited Ballarat in 2009 and was frustrated by his observations. The Gold Rush years which gave birth to Ballarat in the second half of the nineteenth century had been a difficult time. Living conditions were harsh, disasters frequent and murders were common, yet the Gold Rush being presented to tourists was sanitised, emphasising the achievements of a small handful of citizens but ignoring its shadows. Seeing that this blood drenched Goldrush town was without a Ghost Tour he moved to Ballarat and began to establish a ghost-tour enterprise.

Nathaniel had known about the horrors of the asylum system in popular culture from years of reading Lovecraft and Batman, so when he first saw the towering edifice of Aradale with its decaying exterior, labyrinthine corridors, dingy cells and seedy morgue, one thought resounded in his mind: 'Best Ghost Tour Ever.' He later remarked that it was 'As if the ghosts in Aradale saw him at the same time and concluded he was the right man for the job.'

Ghost Tours generally follow a fairly simple formula. A group of people are taken to an historic location, told a carefully scripted story emphasising the horrific nature of what occurred at the sight and detailing incidents of ghostly activity which have been reported. Ghost Tours in Australia face a unique situation. The United Kingdom, Europe and America have centuries of grisly history on which to draw. The further back in history the related events occur the more detached the public are from the story and so there is less likelihood of anyone taking offence because of some personal connection to an element in the story. Australia has far fewer years of history on which to draw and local sensitivities present a veritable minefield which must be taken into consideration. Even Port Arthur, Australia's longest running and most recognisable Ghost Tour located in the nineteenth century ruins of the old convict prison, faced this challenge. The descendants of a 'Hellfire and Brimstone' convict era priest, for example, have challenged the representations of their ancestor and are loud and vocal in their opposition. Portraying a place that incarcerated people with mental illness is far more difficult because often people were interned who had committed no crime; some were victims of injustice and betrayal, some were victims of a system that had no comprehension of their illnesses or distresses, some were simply caught up in a system plagued with internal conflict and under-resourcing. And some were staff, struggling hard to feel that their life work in this place had some ethical justification.

Portraying a convict location with floggings and solitary isolation, is difficult, and mental illness is far more controversial than crime. Therefore, the majority of the script took its influence from the asylum's nineteenth century history. This distanced the script from anyone with more recent connections to the building. Names of all but the most well documented and significant senior officials were omitted to respect anonymity. It also distanced from contemporary notions of offense by presenting a Whiggish narrative when the ill treatment of the past could be set against the progress of the present. This provided the script with a space in time from when many of the most controversial psychiatric practices occurred. Importantly, the introduction of the tour contains a disclaimer regarding the word lunatic, acknowledging that while today it is considered a politically incorrect term, where historically appropriate during the tour it will be used freely and at length. Given that freedom, the guides are taught to relish the word during the tour when applicable to reinforce the socially familiar connotations of horror as often as possible.

It was important that the tour was historically accurate, especially in a rural community with a vibrant and active historical society and community, with many residents having friends and family who either worked or were incarcerated within Aradale's walls. Many hours were spent researching the history of the asylum itself, its place within the wider Australian psychiatric historical landscape, and Australia's position within more global trends and philosophies. Research included rare books written by former psychiatrists who were often both fascinated and appalled by their own industry. In this regard, Dr C. R. D. Brothers seminal work proved invaluable. Official reports such as the 1886 Zox report were scrutinised. Trove proved to be an important resource, as old newspapers gave insights into representations by the media of both mental illness and various scandals during Aradale's asylum period. Where there were gaps, details were filled from books written on other specific lunatic asylums and the asylum system in the British Empire as a whole. Psychiatric journals detailing key psychiatric procedures were consulted when necessary. Foucault and his theories on total institutions were quoted, and the asylum was carefully themed as a machine to grind lunatics into normal people, a theme which reverberates as the central message of the tour. This correlates closely with findings by Holloway who argued that,

> Aligned with this wider development in the tourist industry and with echoes of Dracula Tourism, ghost tourism tends towards the 'lighter' end of the dark tourism spectrum, with entertainment being a key orientation, especially for ghost

> tours. Yet ... this does not preclude moments of sombre reflection and genuine belief and attempts at providing historically accurate portrayals of haunted activity, all of which are usually associated with the 'darkest' form of dark tourism. (Holloway, 2010, 622)

Generally, customers to a ghost tour in a lunatic asylum are familiar with asylum horrors as represented in popular culture and are expecting and seeking to be shocked and disturbed by gory details. The script for the tours drew on a range of sources to find anecdotes of treatments such as bagging, and removal of teeth for biting. Leucotomy, one of the most infamous psychiatric procedures, is given a detailed description and allusions to its history in Aradale are included, despite only circumstantial evidence that they ever occurred on this site. According to reviews on social media, the mortuary is one of the most popular locations on the tour, and extensive research into how autopsies were conducted were utilised when constructing the script. Niceties in the asylum are intentionally omitted in order sit well within the gothic expectations of the public, formulated within a well-established framework of popular culture and scandal.

Ghost tours are different to a traditional historical or heritage tour because they require ghosts as part of the experience. Therefore, a certain amount of poetic licence is permitted, if not indeed required for the tourist experience. The inclusion of ghosts serves to heighten the sense of discomfort and fear for the customer. While sceptics may consider ghosts to be a literary tool useful in storytelling, the inclusion of ghosts in the Aradale tour is a powerful marketing tool exploiting a widely held curiosity on the possibility of paranormal activity. Nathaniel argued that 'if I called it Aradale Night Tour, I would attract a third of the customers.' Folklore regarding ghosts in the asylum did not start with the ghost tour. A few former staff interviewed during the writing process suggested that Aradale had been haunted even when it had been operational. Sightings of the figure of an 1880s dressed 'Nurse Carey' wandering through the Female Ward had been reported by nurses on nightshift up until the asylums closure among numerous other stories.* The description of this figure's clothes imparts historic detail, and does so in a far more engaging way than just a description of historic uniforms. Stories like these were reworded for dramatic impact and included into the script, yet also drew upon established representations in folklore. Key to this is also the importance of the architecture and its archetypal tole in establishing mood and context. As Holloway argues, the materiality of the building itself allows a fertile ground for imaginative play and conjecture, shaped by the liminal space of the tour in its unique architectural context at night, with all the archetypal resonance from that experience.

The tours fundamentally depend on the liminal and interstitial nature of the experience, outside of the normal context of daily life. The focus on windows and doorways, openings to long and ruinous institutional hallways, add a clear architectural and archetypal dimension to the focus on boundaries and thresholds that lie between the realm of the living and the dead. (Kneale, 2006) This sense of boundaries and the out of world experience of the tour, along with the impetus of copious suggestive devices rooted in decades of media experience flowing through the story telling skills of the tour guide, entice the customers to question what lies beyond and to visualize and empathize with the victims of the events of the past. As Holloway argues,

> The ghost story thus has the capacity to present supernatural possibility. Here the story narrative should be read less for its representational qualities and more for what the tale enacts, how it allows space to show up and how it assembles a series of relations that coordinate the ghost tour, as one guide declared, 'I do the stories as if I'm scared by them myself. So hopefully people will empathise with me and think Blimey, he's scared maybe I ought to be scared as well.' (Holloway, 2010, 624)

---

* Personal communication with former staff.

Not all ghosts experiences need to be visual and customers engage with a variety of senses. Ghosts need not be associated with an individual from the past but can represent concentrations of trauma. The script capitalises on both of these premises, and descriptions of customers feeling sick or fainting after being affected by various 'hot spots' such as surgery wards and the mortuary, create a sense of vulnerability; stories of customers physical ghostly experiences such as being scratched or feeling touched elicit particularly notable reactions.

Subtlety in story telling is important. To include dramatic encounters in each room would slowly undermine the potential reality of the supernatural experience for customers. Supposed ghostly encounters are rare; over a two-hour tour guides will tell roughly half a dozen ghost stories and personal stories from guides add another element to the liminal supernatural experience. Anecdotes by guides of encounters experienced while locking up these intimidating building alone after the tours, give the stories and the storyteller a new level of credibility and work to create a supernatural reenchanted place.

The power of suggestion in a location like Aradale at night is enormous. Holloway argues that 'ghost tourism has the capacity to successfully disorientate and open up a sense of possibilities.' (Holloway, 2010, 622) In this, Aradale is highly suited for ghost tours from both historical and architectural angles. The decayed environment of the asylum lends itself perfectly to the atmosphere abetted by the story telling process. The location is huge and multi-levelled, the route of the ghost tour specifically designed to weave in and out, up and down through generic stairwells and corridors that can leave customers lost and disoriented in the dark. The route includes cell blocks lined with solitary cells and darkened corridors branching off in every direction. Wind regularly shakes old windowpanes in an echo reminiscent of footsteps. Doors slam shut when left open; dirty windows cast strange reflections from lanterns; the smell in each room is unique and, depending on the weather, sometimes almost abrasive. Enchantment 'is often a mix, on the one hand, of excitement, awe, and wonder and, on the other, of unease, dislocation and unpredictability.' (Holloway, 2010,

263) The goal of the tour is to exploit the architecture so as to enchant the customer with the possibility of paranormal experience.

The result is a gothic, haunting script that acknowledges the borders between sanity and insanity, life and death are often subjective. It is also an experience which balances on a tightrope between historicity and the well-established archetypes of horror and gothic fiction. Customers who already believe in the supernatural have their beliefs reinforced and sceptics perhaps leave with their beliefs challenged. All leave emotionally affected and this both spreads the notion that ghosts are real and that the asylum is an 'enchanted space' on the boundaries of the real and supernatural world. It also challenges the participants with the experience of tragedy surrounding the history of mental illness. If the integrity of anything in the asylum is criticised it is the system itself and what it has come to represent in the popular imagination.

Marketing has to reflect the dark aspect of the asylum so pictures for webpages and promotional shots were taken at night. Interviews and media releases highlighted the death rate and key terms such as 'Australia's most haunted building' were reiterated. As state and national media became aware of Aradale, sections included discussion about the ghosts of the asylum amid a flurry of newspaper articles discussing the newfound notoriety of the building as a 'haunted site'. International recognition arrived after an episode of *Ghost Hunters: International* featured Aradale and was aired in at least nine countries.

In America, where the remains of at least one large and decrepit former mental hospital can be found in nearly every state, but also in England, there has been a backlash against the use of such facilities for haunted themed tourism.

> Such representations have drawn criticism from disability advocates on the basis that they perpetuate stereotypes and inaccurately represent the history of deinstitutionalisation in the United States. (George, 2014, 4)

Despite precautions to observe respectabilities, sensitivities, and historical accuracy, local reaction to the opening of the Aradale Ghost Tours was less than favourable. The then Mayor of Ararat was quoted in the local newspaper exclaiming that she was personally disgusted and would hold a public forum to listen to community concerns. Many locals refused to be involved and simply concluded that this was a case of an individual exploiting personal tragedy to make a profit. The Day Tours were being conducted by local volunteers, also eager to keep memory of the asylum alive and these also took a similar negative stance towards the Ghost Tours. Many of the volunteers had historical connections with Aradale, some being former staff or relatives of former staff, others eager to distance previous generations from controversial histories which they feared might find their way into a ghost tour. Operating within the not-for-profit organisation Friends of J Ward, they had maintained the J Ward facility of the asylum for the criminally insane since its closure, and more recently included a museum, funded by the tours they had been conducting. These tours presented a sanitised version of the asylum's history, omitting the difficult and tragic aspects and focusing on anecdotes and fond memories deemed suitable for families. Amongst these volunteers there was a feeling that any commercial enterprise, and particularly a Ghost Tour focusing on the horrors of the asylum, must be purely exploitative. There was also a strong concern to present a positive representation of the site to offset the impact of the severely critical 1991 inquiry into abuse at Aradale which led to the asylum's closure. These differences over representations of the asylum's history clashed and resulted in a rift that still exists between day and night tour organizations.

This clash is not unique. Pennhurst Asylum, located in Pennsylvania was a massive 4,000 bed mental facility which, like Aradale, closed in the late 1980s and 90s following decades of reported abuses against patients. Following its closure local residents and former staff created the Pennhurst Memorial and Preservation Society, aimed at keeping the memory and as much of the facility as possible intact. Members of the society became publicly outraged when the asylum was purchased by a businessman named Richard Chakenjian. The Preservation Society, torn between a new owner keen to restore and maintain parts of the asylum and the fear that their sanitized narrative might be challenged by a well-funded business model, suggested the new owner could do less damage to their narrative by presenting an alternative perspective focused on vampires and monsters rather than psychiatry and the spirits of tormented patients. (Beitiks, 2012) Initially a compromise was reached in which a narrative involving a fictional 'Dr. Chakenjian' took groups through the asylum, regaling them with a blend of history, folklore and pure fantasy, but in time the perception of Pennhurst and its problematic history was too entrenched to be ignored in these representations. Visitors to the asylum wanted to engage with the historical context of the Pennhurst Asylum and they demanded ghosts, not vampires. They wanted a sense of authenticity incorporating the more macabre aspects of the asylum's history. The Pennhurst Asylum webpage currently lists not only a variety of highly theatrical horror tours featuring bloodied nurses leading groups past displays of horrific experiments in the mortuary, it also features an extensive list of historical ghost tours and paranormal investigation tours tied to Pennhurst's history. (https://pennhurstasylum.com/).

A similar dynamic has been present in the Aradale site. Seeing the commercial success of the Aradale Ghost Tours, the Friends of J Ward have accommodated the power of the ghostly and now contract another company to run ghost tours with escape rooms where tourists pretend to be patients trapped within the facility in the J Ward section of the Ararat Lunatic Asylum.

Despite the controversy, the Aradale Ghost Tours has proved extremely popular, primarily with people from Melbourne curious as to the history and heritage of the asylum and with a desire to explore such an infamous liminal site, but also with a large core of enthusiasts who were willing to travel considerable distances to finally walk the 'haunted corridors' of the asylum and encounter ghosts. In its first year of operation, six thousand people made the journey to explore the Asylum via the ghost tours. That figure has now grown to an average of nearly twenty thousand per year. The tours originally employed two guides and one administrator. At the time of writing, there are eight guides, one administrator and one bookings officer.

The tours have evolved. The most popular is the two-hour ghost tour, heavily inspired by European ghost tours. Paranormal investigation tours followed and these catered to smaller groups and included more time in each location and in the asylum in general, with the advantage of a collection of instruments used by paranormal investigation television shows to find evidence of the ghostly. Emulating a growing number of 'paranormal reality television' shows such as *Ghost Adventures* and *Ghost Hunters*, these tours, modelled on Victorian seances, engage in a modern paranormal investigation which involves asking questions to the environment and beyond in the hope of receiving a supernatural response (Sabol, 2015). The modern paranormal investigation frequently involves the use of various devices such as electromagnetic field detectors normally used by electricians to detect current, night vision goggles and laser thermometers. An industry of paranormal investigation equipment has evolved to cater to enthusiasts and utilises many examples of this pseudo-scientific technological apparatus. Entire buildings are set up with night vision CCTV cameras which patrons can monitor in the hope of spotting orbs or other supposed supernatural activity. Sometimes the equipment does give off readings; satellites passing overhead give off radio signals that can be detected by the equipment, much of which is designed for other purposes yet thousands of people each year leave Aradale with their belief in ghosts validated by the equipment's flashing lights and audible signals. The patrons also leave having had an engagement with the asylums past, albeit one mediated through technology and a liminal space of supernaturalism and re-enchantment.

Folklore concerning Aradale has developed separately from the script. Ghost tour patrons who already have firm beliefs in the paranormal have found their belief validated on the tour and regularly express their experiences to guides, family and friends This not only achieves word-of-mouth advertising for the various tours but it also spreads new stories of paranormal activity that customers may in turn be inclined to experience while touring the asylum.

Operating such tours in a deteriorating building comes with a range of complications and challenges. Maintenance is a burden on the owners and regularity has been interrupted twice in the nine years since the tours began as a result of occupational health and safety concerns. Sleep-over tours operated for a short time and proved to be very successful, attracting a significant international audience, however the building is still registered as a hospital and hospitals, by law, require operational smoke alarms and electronic exit signs connected to backup generators, systems which had long since fallen into disrepair. Four years later, when low-level lead contamination from old paint was detected onsite, all staff were required to provide blood test results annually. Ongoing maintenance issues are a consistent problem as government departments struggle to find funds and justification for spending on the site. Nevertheless, the ghost tours have become an important part of the local tourism economy. Accommodation, restaurants and other tourism providers have all benefited from the transition from psychiatric hospital to haunted house. Every time the ghost tour has been threatened the community has rallied behind attempts to resolve the issues. For some, the ghost tour has become a necessary evil.

8

Conclusion

> Sitting on top of what was coined as Madman's Hill, the grounds of Ararat were said to be beautiful.
>
> White, stately and tree-lined, the Victorian, 'Italiante' architecture is also a reminder of a time when archaic attitudes to mental health ruled, and treatments like leucotomies, straitjackets and the then underdeveloped and at times dangerous use of electro-convulsive shock therapy were the norm.
>
> Whether or not you believe in the paranormal, one thing is certain – that even without its suspected ghosts and supernatural occurrences, the history of Ararat Mental Asylum is most definitely haunted.
>
> (https://www.mamamia.com.au/ararat-mental-asylum-australias-haunted-building/)

In 2017, Aradale Ghost Tours became the first dark tourism project to be recognised with a Victorian Tourism Award in the Cultural Tourism category, coming alongside the internationally recognised State Library of Victoria and the Port of Echuca Discovery Centre. This helped bring more attention from state government officials who also became fascinated with the building and offered support. Keeping the building intact relies on how much it is used and so discussions for further uses of the Aradale site will continue. All suggestions have encountered difficulties. No one has come forward with a desire to purchase the property and the annual maintenance costs alone are enormous. The Heritage listing of Aradale's sister asylum, Willsmere, saved the exterior from the developer's bulldozer. Its location in the centre of Kew is highly sort after real estate and the former lunatic asylum has been converted into luxury accommodation for some of the city's affluent. Ararat, however, is a small town in a very rural locality, over two hours drive from the Melbourne and so is not appropriate for a similar conversion to luxury apartments. To date, no party has offered any workable usage of the site beyond dark tourism, and given the growing reputation of Aradale as 'Australia's most haunted site', the ghost tour has become an integral part of the future of the former asylum.

Ghost tours generally, and the ghost tour at Aradale in particular, highlight the fact that some people not only like to be scared but also have a curiosity about ghosts and there seems to permeate the psyche of humanity a desire to encounter something else, something inexplicable in terms of ordinary physics and logic. Jungian analyst James Hollis argues that this sense of being 'haunted', of ghostly experiences is fundamentally a psychic projection generated by the deeper suppressed workings of a person's psychological state within their broader social and cultural context. He argues that we are all influenced by the presence of invisible forms, spirits, parental influences, dreams and impulses as a reflection of the untold stories, synchronicities and complexes which permeate us in our lived social experience. The framework he proposes indicates that a 'ghostly' experience, whether it is encountered as an event which comes upon a person unbidden or even as a deliberately perpetrated falsehood, is nevertheless an indicator of much deeper stirrings in the psyche of the individual within his or her cultural context. Ghosts, in whatever manifestation they are encountered, are a window into the internal workings of the society and the individual. (Hollis, 2014, 84)

Carl Jung theorised that the more anxiety resides within the unconscious the more it is likely to generate negative and traumatic impacts on the psyche. The unconscious aspect of a person's or community's psyche can only be utilised positively if there is a conscious recognition and expression of its existence and an integration of this comprehended reality into functional operations, individually and corporately. For this to occur, the individual or community must acknowledge the content of the unconscious, encounter it, live it and suffer it. The power of the unconscious is problematic if it remains unacknowledged and silenced. The buried aspects of the psyche will find ways of signifying and making known their suppressed content; they will erupt into the conscious life in an unmediated and often violent way, unless integrated.

Aradale's haunted past is arguably the unconscious eruption of the hidden-ness of its unnamed traumas. The strength of this haunted urban imagination is the direct counterpart to the obfuscation of the institution's violent heritage. In the psyche of the individual and/or community, the phenomenon of ghosts and spectres is a kind of 'entanglement' between history and the unconscious which is given expression through experiences connected to unsettlement, displacement, transgression, repressed anxiety and loss of security. On behalf of the community, ghosts and paranormal activity enact the fear, the displacement, the dislocation and the unspoken. As the ghost researcher John Sabol argues,

> What emerges (or materializes) is a re-assemblage of what still remains; the 'ghost'. The use of a creative experiential, entangled, and relational archaeology in the present can engage in those spaces in which the past intervenes today in the present 'haunted sites'. (Sabol, 2013, 10)

For Freud, uncanny experiences occur when the comforting and familiar become entangled with the strange, rendering them both familiar and alienated. In this experience there occurs a duality in which one has a sense of being in and out of place at the same time. In an experience of haunting, this dichotomy characterises precisely the moment when repressed tensions and anxieties of the past return to haunt the present. Ghost stories fulfil the function of storytelling; they recall the past and its meaning into the present and its meaning. Ghost stories and supernatural mysteries proliferated in the tumultuous history of Aradale, and they continue today because of their role in memorialising traumatic experiences aided and abetted by the medium of storytelling. The history needs to be told and told again until the bleak past is made known and resolved.

Part of the appeal of these tours is the extensive use of asylums as a locus of horror in popular culture, featuring extensively in gothic horror novels, films, computer games and television programs. However, underlying this appeal is the use of ghosts, dark history and folklore as a vehicle for memorializing trauma in communities. This is clearly reflected in the case of the use of the Ararat Lunatic Asylum as a site of 'dark tourism'; albeit integrated in the wider spectrum of lunacy and asylums as sites of horror both in terms of tales of abuse and neglect within the asylum system as well as fear of the lunatics themselves as potential perpetrators of horror in popular culture.

However, while this is certainly the case pertaining to the folklore surrounding ghosts and ghost stories within communities, there are tensions with this hypothesis when the process of the haunting experience is mediated (and motivated) by a consumer-based industry deriving representations from popular culture and local history. There is also the danger of relegating the experience of the voiceless to that of an objectified vicarious freak show for public consumption. In a sense, both the positive and negative representations of the site, as demonstrated by the Friends of J Ward and the 'dark tourism' industry, maintain the voicelessness of the oppressed and, in a sense, objectify their experiences for the purview of others within a polarized discourse of 'madness'. In neither case do we hear the voices of those who were patients and those who were targeted by the use of asylums as a vehicle for social control.

The issue of representation of the disenfranchised is particularly pertinent when examining the legacy of a site like 'the Ararat Lunatic

Asylum', now referred to as Aradale. These sites are contested in that they pertain to the interests of diverse segments of society yet their heritage management and status is determined within the context of established hierarchies of power. In this case, the representation of Aradale as a heritage site is quite removed from the life experiences of the patients who were its primary recipients. It is particularly telling that Aradale achieved legal status as a heritage site on 21 March 1978, on the grounds that:

> Aradale Mental Hospital is a landmark in Ararat. It has played a strong role in the history of this city and is particularly important architecturally. Although similarly planned and detailed to the contemporary Beechworth and later Kew Asylums, the use of the linking bridges with an arcade on an arched gateway is unique and particularly important. The towers and detailing of the central block are distinctive. The asylum is an important example of Italianate conservative Classical design ... As an example of a very large scale government institution, for its imposing yet functional architecture and comprehensive planning, for its associations with the evolving provision of mental health services from the middle of the nineteenth century. (Dep't of Environment, 2015)

Western attitudes toward human rights are clear about the responsibility of society to protect its living vulnerable members – they have been enshrined in written form as the Universal Declaration of Human Rights. Under the conventions expressed therein tourism in a functioning mental health facility along the lines of the 'gawkers' at Bedlam would be considered a legal impossibility and would invoke an immediate moral outrage. Less clear, though equally important, are attitudes about the responsibility of society to protect the rights of its dead vulnerable members. While a precise set of rules prevent the mistreatment of physical remains, the memories and other traces that linger post mortem are not so well protected. Laws surrounding defamation of character describe specific instances in which living descendants may litigate because the alleged offence has caused them harm; but these laws do not expressly apply to the deceased person who was actually defamed. Beyond this, the most distinct legal protection for the deceased inhabitants of former asylums lies in the careful sealing of records for a prescribed time after death. Varied cultural practices concerning death seem to impede society from achieving a consensus about how to treat the intangible remnants of the dead.

A challenge here for historians is how to manage inherently complex responsibilities towards representations of the dead. One way to consider this is in relation to conventions surrounding the living; expressing a clear understanding that the responsibilities for redressing abuses against the dead outweigh the rights of the living individuals to pick and choose what memories and histories are articulated by society collectively. In this sense, memory and history are necessary conditions for society to discharge their responsibilities to the dead in terms of the legacy of trauma across generations and the responsibility we have towards reconciling ourselves towards that legacy.

As a monument of national significance, conservation management plans will be largely guided by Australia ICOMOS Incorporated's *Burra Charter*. (ICOMOS Inc, 2013) Given the reason for Aradale's heritage listing has a heavy bias toward the architecture of the buildings, following the *Charter* would lead to an interpretation of the site that strongly favours the physical over the intangible. This creates a potential tension between the stated heritage conservation intentions and the interests of large numbers of visitors to the site – exacerbating the already problematic situation of the voicelessness of the oppressed. (Winkworth, 2005, 48–50) Such issues of focus of interpretation are typically dealt with through considering the relative degrees of significance of values applied to a heritage site, yet, as of August 2015, there were no official heritage values assigned to Aradale.

> Conservation involves an inherent dilemma. It embraces both use and preservation. Yet use can lead to destruction.

> For managers, the hardest planning decision is concerning the extent to which the goals of preservation or protection constrain those relating to human use and enjoyment of the heritage place? [*sic*] Numerous considerations make the decision palatable for resource managers. The extent of the resource, its significance, rarity, and existing status are value-laden factors, but provide the basis of a defensible rationale for adopting a particular use-preservation balance. (Carter & Grimwade, 1997, 45)

For those in authority having to justify their decisions to a budget-conscious public, perhaps the most fiscally responsible usage of a site like Aradale is to allow it to disappear from the landscape. Following the example of the former Yarra Bend Lunatic Asylum of Melbourne, the removal of existing infrastructure would make it possible to utilise the valuable land for more profitable purposes. (Bonwick, 1996) Alternatively, the buildings might be saved through re-purposing and redevelopment that considers the integrity of the architecture, if not the integrity of the intangible heritage. Either treatment requires a complete historical disassociation of the space and the people who were once its inhabitants. ('Inhabitants' referring here not just to the inmates but all those associated with Aradale.) Be it for the purpose of serious education or titillating entertainment, tourism to the site requires the very opposite. It is impossible to tell the history (an apparently truthful account of the past) or live the heritage (a popular accounting that occurs through storytelling and shared experiences) of the space without the inclusion of people. Aradale is not just a collection of bricks and mortar sitting atop a hill. (Vogler, 2007, 95–7) Nor is it just a symbol of past practices of institutionalisation that may now seem impossible to comprehend. Though no longer operational, the asylum maintains an integral importance in the memories of the living. For this reason, monetary arguments justifying preservation and protection judgments tend to be viewed by the broader public as a gross misrepresentation of the significance of sites like Aradale. (Carter & Grimwade, 1997, 45–53)

Perhaps by re-focusing their justifications from economics to people, those in authority will find the public more responsive to the decisions taken.

One danger of this development though, is the necessary subordination of the existing tourism activities to the integrity of the site. (Carter & Bramley, 2002, 187) There are also concerns regarding the preservation of the symbolic and historical authenticity of the site given the pressures of enormous maintenance costs, changing regulations pertaining to health and safety and wear and tear of increased tourism. These costs and the accompanying legal ramifications are already creating serious tensions between the stake holders with investment in the site as a tourist destination.* To a large extent the primary impetus to engage in maintenance and preservation of the site financially is driven by the financial success of the ghost tour industry which has led to tensions regarding cultural ownership of the site and the iconic question of control over representations of the mentally ill in Australian heritage.

In Australia little work has been done to define society's relationship to such heritage sites as Aradale. There is a dearth of well-informed literature to help determine the future directions for defunct asylums. Looking internationally, policies in the United Kingdom and New Zealand reflect disparate social expectations for reuse of the sites. (Alun, Kearns & Moon, 2010, 148) In the UK sentiments arise from a national desire for limited memorialisation of the former use of buildings while ensuring that communities benefit from retention of the built infrastructure, resulting in replication of successful redevelopment projects. For the New Zealand public the arguments remain entrenched at a local level, occasioning a case-by-case decision making process. In all circumstances the former asylums are isolated spaces that resist integration into today's communities, even though their names loom large in the collective memory. (Cornish, 1997, 105; Alun, Kearns & Moon, 2009, 81) This is a memory of a haunting stigma that imbues these sites with a negative brand that can only fail to interpret the 'complex set of meanings associated with the site'. (Deacon,

---

* Personal communication with representatives of the Friends of J Ward and Eerie Tours.

2004, 313) These overseas examples demonstrate how a 'limited collective will to materialize remembrance in an overt manner' has created a sense of having to overcome the stigma of the former asylum sites in order to re-use them. Perhaps ironically though, it is in this very stigma that the funds for the preservation and protection of Aradale will ultimately be derived. (Kearns, Alun & Moon, 2010, 744)

These questions are particularly pertinent when examining the problem of authenticity in representations regarding the experiences of those who lived within the institution and the desire for tourist markets to have visiting experiences which fit within popular representations of asylums in fiction and local community ownership of a site. This indicates the importance of balancing the interests of stake holders in a community and the importance of continued negotiation and recognition of the sensitivity of a complex like Aradale as a site of social conscience. The re-branding of Aradale as a site of conscience would increase the focus of future conservation management plans on the intangible values. It would also raise the primary significance to the international level, creating new opportunities for development of visitor numbers which could be incorporated within the established infrastructure of stake holders and already financially successful tourist and community organizations.

Bibliography

Alun, J., Kearns, R., Moon, G. (2010) 'Memorialisation and remembrance: on strategic forgetting and the metamorphosis of psychiatric asylums into sites for tertiary educational provision.' *Social & Cultural Geography*. 11, no. 8, 731–49.

Aradale Ghost Tours (Social Media), https://www.facebook.com/AradaleGhostTours/.

Aradale: Victorian Heritage Data Base, https://vhd.heritagecouncil.vic.gov.au/places/28.

Ararat Asylum, Australia's Most Haunted Building, https://www.mamamia.com.au/ararat-mental-asylum-australias-haunted-building/.

Ashton, P. and Wilson, J. (2014) *Silent Systems: Forgotten Australians and the Institutionalization of Women and Children*. Australian Scholarly Publishing: Melbourne.

Avery, G. (2008) *Ghostly Matters: Haunting and the sociological imagination*, Minnesota, Minnesota University Press.

Baastrup, P. C., Poulsen, J. C., Schou, M., Thomsen, K., & Amdisen, A. (1970) 'Prophylactic lithium: double blind discontinuation in manic-depressive and recurrent-depressive disorders.' *The Lancet*, 296(7668), 326–30.

Bartlett, P. (1993) 'The poor law of lunacy: the administration of pauper lunatics in mid-nineteenth century England, with special emphasis on Leicestershire and Rutland'. Doctoral dissertation, University of London.

Basso, K. H. (1996) *Wisdom Sits in Places: Landscape and language among the Western Apache*. UNM Press: Albuquerque.

Bedlam House, https://tvtropes.org/pmwiki/pmwiki.php/Main/BedlamHouse, accessed 1.10.2019.

Beitiks, E. S. (2012) 'The ghosts of institutionalization at Pennhurst's Haunted Asylum'. Hastings Center Report, 42(1), 22–4.

Bircanon & Sturt (1886) 'Glimpses of the Past', North East Psychiatry Services.

Bonwick, R. (1996) 'The History of Yarra Bend Lunatic Asylum, Melbourne'. Masters Research Thesis, Department of Psychiatry, University of Melbourne.

Bostock, J. (1968) 'The dawn of Australian psychiatry: an account of the measures taken for the care of mental invalids from the time of the First Fleet, 1788, to the year 1850, including a survey of the overseas background and the case notes of Dr F. Campbell (No. 4).' Australian Medical Association.

Bower, Herbert, interviewed by Belinda Robson, 7 March 1997. Bower was born 19th December 1914 in Vienna. He was at the Launceston General Hospital in Tasmania from 1947 to 1949. WWIA 1968.

Brontë, Charlotte (2000) *Jane Eyre*. OUP, Oxford.

Brothers, C. R. D. (1957) *Early Victorian Psychiatry, 1835–1905*. A.C. Brooks, Govt. Printer, Melbourne.

Brown, Theo (1982) *Devon Ghosts*. Norwich, Jarrold Publishing.

Cade, John (1949) 'Lithium Salts in the Treatment of Psychotic Excitement', *Medical Journal of Australia*, Vol. 2

Cade, John (1979) *Mending the Mind: A Short History of Twentieth Century Psychiatry*, Melbourne, Sun Books.

Carpenter, M. (1980) *Re-Writing Nursing History*, Richmond, Croom Helm Publishers.

Carter, Bill and Grimwade, Gordon (1997) 'Balancing use and preservation in cultural heritage management.' *International Journal of Heritage Studies*. 3, no. 1: 45–53.

Carter, R. and Bramley. R. (2002) 'Defining Heritage Values and Significance for Improved Resource Management: an application to Australian tourism.' *International Journal of Heritage Studies*. 8, no. 3: 175–99.

Clarke, P.A. (2007) 'Indigenous Spirit and Ghost Folklore of "Settled" Australia', *Folklore*, Vol. 118. No. 2.

Connolly, A. (2003) 'Psychoanalytic theory in times of terror'. *Journal of Analytical Psychology*, 48(4), 407–31.

Cornish, C. (1997) 'Behind the crumbling walls; the re-working of a former asylum's geography'. *Health & Place* 3, no. 2: 101–10.

Davies, O. (2007) *The Haunted: A social history of ghosts*. Palgrave Macmillan.

Dax, C. (1949) 'Review of exhibition of patients' artwork from Netherne Hospital.' *British Medical Journal*, 23.

Dax, C. (1953) *Experimental Studies in Psychiatric Art*, London, Faber & Faber.

Dax, C. (1961) *From Asylum to Community*, Melbourne, Canberra, Sydney, Cheshire.

Dax, C. (1981). 'Crimes, follies and misfortunes in the history of Australasian psychiatry'. *Australian & New Zealand Journal of Psychiatry*, 15(3), 257–63.

Dax, C. (1998) *Mental Health in my Lifetime; In John Best, Portraits in Australian Health*, Sydney, MacLennan and Petty.

Dax, C. (1947) *Modern Mental Treatment: A Handbook for Nurses*, London, Faber and Faber.

Dax, C. (1992) 'The Evolution of Community Psychiatry', *Australian & New Zealand Journal of Psychiatry*, 26(2), 295–301.

Dax, C. et al (1948) 'Prefrontal Leucotomy: a review', Netherne Hospital Surrey.

Deacon, H. (2004) 'Intangible Heritage in Conservation Management Planning: The Case of Robben Island.' *International Journal of Heritage Studies*. 10, no. 3: 309–19.

Dickson, Diane (2013) 'The Land of Rainbows', Master's thesis, University of Melbourne.

Dunk, J. (2019) *Bedlam at Botany Bay*. Sydney, NSW: New South Publishing, UNSW Press Ltd.

Edwards, K. (1997) 'Four Cases of Prefrontal Leucotomy', *Medical Journal of Australia*. 2

Ellery, R.S. (1955) *The Cow Jumped Over the Moon: Private Papers of a Psychiatrist*, Melbourne.

Jentsch, Ernst (1906) 'Zur Psychologie des Unheimlichen (kommentiert) Erstveröffentlichung' in: *Psychiatrisch – Neurologische Wochenschrift*. Nr. 822, 823.

Fessler, A. (1956) 'The Management of Lunacy in Seventeenth Century England. An Investigation of Quarter-Sessions Records.' *Proceedings of the Royal Society of Medicine*, vol 49, 901–7.

Fewster, G. (1950) Mental Hygiene Authority Bill, Victorian Legislative assembly, 1 November 1950, p. 1808.

Foote, K. E. (2003) *Shadowed Ground: America's landscapes of violence and tragedy*. University of Texas Press.

Foucault, M. (1967) *Madness and Civilization: a history of insanity in the Age of Reason*. London: Tavistock.

Fox, Charles. 'Forehead low, aspect idiotic: Intellectual disability in Victorian Asylums, 1870–1887', in MacKinnon, D and Colebrook, C. (2002)

Madness in Australia: History, Heritage and the Asylum. University of Queensland Press: St Lucia.

Freud, S. 'The Uncanny' in *The Penguin Freud Library*, vol. 14: Art and Literature, ed. Richard Wollheim. Harmondsworth, 1990, 339–76.

Furse, A. (2014) 'Hospital Drama: Visual Theatres of the Medical Rendezvous from Asylum to Hospital with Reference to Specific Works by Anna Furse'. *Interdisciplinary Science Reviews, 39*(3), 238–57.

George, K. (2014) *The Birth of a Haunted 'Asylum': Public memory and community storytelling*. Temple University.

Giese, J. (2018) *The Maddest Place on Earth*. Australian Scholarly Publishing: Melbourne.

Gilman, S. (1987) 'The struggle of psychiatry with psychoanalysis: who won?' *Critical Inquiry, 13*(2), 293–313.

Goffman, E. (1990) *Asylums: essays on the social situation of mental patients and other inmates*. New York: Doubleday.

Gordon, A. (2008) *Ghostly Matters: Haunting and the sociological imagination*, Minneapolis, University of Minneapolis.

Gresswell, D. Astley (Dan Astley) & Victoria. Board of Public Health (1891) Report by Dr Gresswell on the sanitary condition of the Borough of Ararat: and on the prevalence of typhoid fever and fatal throat illness in the Ararat Lunatic Asylum. Govt. Printer, Melbourne

Holloway, J. (2010) 'Legend-tripping in spooky spaces: ghost tourism and infrastructures of enchantment.' *Environment and Planning D: Society and Space* 28, no. 4. 618–37.

Hariman, R., & Lucaites, J. (2008) 'Public identity and collective memory in US iconic photography', in *Visual rhetoric: A reader in communication and American culture*, 175–98.

Hollis, J. (2014, April). Hauntings. In Workshop: Saturday.

Hooper-Greenhill, E. (2007) 'Interpretive communities, strategies and repertoires'. *Museums and Their Communities*, 76–94.

Hunt, I. H. (1851) *Astounding Disclosures!: Three Years in a Mad House: a True Account of the Barbarous, Inhuman and Cruel Treatment of Isaac H. Hunt, in the Maine Insane Hospital...* AA Mann.

Hunter, R., & Macalpine, I. (1974) *Psychiatry for the poor: 1851 Colney Hatch Asylum – Friern Hospital 1973: a medical and social history*. Dawsons Pall Mall.

ICOMOS Australia Incorporated (2013) The Burra Charter. https://australia.icomos.org/.

Jameson, F. (1991) *Postmodernism, or, the cultural logic of late capitalism*. Duke university Press.

Jenkins, H. (2003) Transmedia Storytelling. Technology Review. Revista del Massachusetts Institute of Technology (MIT), 4.

Jones, K. (1972) *Law and Conscience Lunacy. A history of the mental health services*. London: Routledge and Kegan Paul, 198–212.

Jung, C. (1960) *The Collected Works of C.G. Jung*, Volume 3: Psychogenesis of Mental Disease (Adler, G., & Hull, R., eds.). Princeton, N. J.: Princeton University Press.

Jung, C. (1968) *Archetypes of the Collective Unconscious* (R. F. C. Hull, Trans.). In H. Read et al. (eds.), *The Collected Works of C. G. Jung* (Vol. 9 pt. 1, 2nd edn., pp. 3–41). Princeton, N. J.: Princeton University Press.

Jung, C. (1969) *Analytical Psychology and 'Weltanschauung'*. In Adler G. & Hull R. (eds.), *The Collected Works of C.G. Jung*, Volume 8: Structure & Dynamics of the Psyche (pp. 358–81). Princeton, N. J.: Princeton University Press.

Jung, C. (1970) *Mysterium Coniunctionis* (R. F. C. Hull, Trans.) (H. Read et al., eds.), *The Collected Works of C. G. Jung* (Vol. 14, 2nd edn.). Princeton, N. J.: Princeton University Press.

Jung, C. (1982) *The Collected Works of C.G. Jung*, Volume 16: Practice of Psychotherapy (Adler, G., & Hull, R., eds.). Princeton, N. J.: Princeton University Press.

King, S. (1981) *Danse Macabre*, Hodder Paperback, New York. 1981.

Kneale, J. (2006) 'From beyond: H. P. Lovecraft and the place of horror', *Cultural Geographies* 13, 106–26.

Luckins, Tanya 'Crazed with grief', in MacKinnon, D., & Coleborne, C. (2002). *Madness in Australia: histories, heritage and the asylum*. University of Queensland Press: St Lucia.

McDonald, D. I. (1971) 'Dr Francis Campbell of Tarban Creek Asylum'. *Medical Journal of Australia*, 1(1), 39–41.

McEwan, C. (2008) 'A very modern ghost: postcolonialism and the politics of enchantment.' *Environment and Planning D: Society and Space*, 26(1), 29–46.

MacKinnon, D., & Colebrook, C. (2002) *Madness in Australia: History, Heritage and the Asylum*. University of Queensland Press: St Lucia.

MacKinnon, Dolly (2002) 'Introduction', in Mackinnon, D and Colebourne, C. (2002) *Madness in Australia: Histories, Heritage and the Asylum*. University of Queensland Press, St Lucia.

McPhee, Peter (1995) *Pansy: A life of Roy Douglas Wright*, Melbourne, Melbourne University Press.

Mental Hygiene Authority Act, 1950 section 10.

Miller, J. (1961) 'The Myth of Mental Illness: Foundations of A Theory of

Personal Conduct.' *American Journal of Psychoanalysis*, 21(2), 302–8. Thomas S. Szasz, MD Harper, New York.

Monk, L. A. (2007) 'Made enquiries, can elicit no history of injury: Researching the history of institutional abuse in the archives'. *Provenance*, (6), 42.

Monk, L. A. (2008) *Attending madness: At work in the Australian colonial asylum,* Vol. 84. Rodopi.

Newton, J. (2019) 'Symbolic Faces of Mullawallah' in Wickam, D., & Gevasoni, C. (ed.) *Pay Dirt! Ballarat and Other Gold Towns*, BHS Publishing, Ballarat.

Nichol, D. MacKinnon, D. and Reeves, K. Goldfields, 'Asylums and Anxieties', in Reeves, K., & Nichols, D. (2007) *Deeper Leads*. Ballarat Heritage Services, Ballarat.

Owens, S. (2017) *The Ghost: A Cultural History*. Tate Publishing: London.

Parkinson, J. P. (1981) 'The castle hill lunatic asylum (1811–1826) and the origins of eclectic pragmatism in Australian psychiatry.' *Australian and New Zealand Journal of Psychiatry*, 15(4), 319–22.

Patrick, V. et al (2006) 'Facilitating Discharge to State Psychiatric Institutions: a group intervention strategy', *Psychiatric Rehabilitation Journal*, 29.1

Pennhurst Asylum, https://pennhurstasylum.com/.

Pinel, P. (1806) *A treatise on insanity*. London, United Kingdom: Messers Cadell & Davies, Strand.

Real Paranormal Experiences, https://realparanormalexperiences.com/ararat-lunatic-asylum-the-haunting

Rollason, B. (2017) 'A rare insight into the unique history of Victoria's first hospital for the mentally ill', https://www.abc.net.au/news/2017-10-21/looking-back-in-time-at-ararats-mental-asylum/9072024, accessed 16.06.2019.

Rubenstein, W. D., & Rubenstein, H. L. *Menders of the Mind: A History of the Australian and New Zealand College of Psychiatry 1946–1996*, Melbourne, Oxford University Press.

Sabol, John (2015) *Haunting Presences, Ruins, and Ghostly Entanglements: Excavations at the Edge of Performance*, Charleston, SC, Amazon Digital Services.

Sachdev, P., & Sachdev, J. (2005) 'Long term out comes of neurosurgery for the treatment of depression', *Journal of Neuropsychiatry and Neuroscience.*

Sagan, C. (1980) *Cosmos*, New York, Random House Publishing.

Sands, N. (2009) 'Round the Bend: A Brief History of Mental Health Nursing in Victoria, Australia 1848 to 1950's', *Issues in Mental Health*

Nursing, 30:6, 364–71.

Scull, A. (1978) *Museums of Madness: The Social Organisation of Society in 19th Century England*, London, Allen Lane.

Scull, A. (1993) *The Most Solitary of Afflictions: madness and society in Britain, 1700–1900*. Yale University Press.

Segal, C. (1983) *Cosmos,* Auckland, Abacus Books.

Shipley, T. Ed. (1961) *Classics in Psychology*. Philosophical Library: New York.

Showalter, E. (1985) *The Female Malady: Madness and English Culture*, New York, Pantheon Books.

Smith, L. D. (1995) 'The Great Experiment: The Place of Lincoln in the History of Psychiatry'. *Lincolnshire History and Archaeology*, 30, 55–62.

Sneadr, Walter (2005) *Drug Discovery: a history*, Chichester, Wiley.

Stoller, Alan (1981) 'The First Decade', in Jerzy Krupinski; Alan Mackenzie and Rachelle Banchevska (ed.) *Psychiatric Research in Victoria*, Mental Health Research Institute, Health Commission of Victoria.

Szaasz, T. (1961) *The Myth of Mental Illness: Foundations of a Theory of personal Conduct*, London, Secker

Tether, Leah (1917) *Publishing the Grail, in Medieval and Renaissance France*, Suffolk, D. S. Brewer.

Thorkild, Jacobsen (1975) *The Treasure of Darkness: A history of Mesopotamian Religion*, Connecticut, Yale University Press.

Thomas. S. MD Harper, New York, 1961. *American Journal of Psychoanalysis*, 21(2), 302–8.

Toy, Mitchell (2014) Victorian psychiatric patients' grim fate in hellish 1800s hospitals,https://www.heraldsun.com.au/news/victoria/victorian-psychiatric-patients-grim-fate-in-hellish-1800s-hospitals/news-story/c7928ebe8a9f527a941cce86e0990fef.

Trigg, D. (2016) 'An Insect Trapped in Amber: the Flesh of a Ghost', in Olson, D. (ed.), *Guillermo del Toro's The Devil's Backbone and Pan' Labyrinth: Studies in the Horror Film* (Colorado: Centipede Press), pp. 69–87.

Van der Kolk, S., & Coenraad, J. L. (1870) *The Pathology and Therapeutics of Mental Diseases*. John Churchill & sons.

Victorian Legislative Assembly, 31 October 1950.

Vogler, Agnes (2007) 'Forging heritage for the tourist gaze: Australian history and contemporary representations reviewed.' *Journal of Australian Studies*. 31, no. 91: 93–106.

VPARL 1988–92, no. 198 The investigative Task Force Findings on the Aradale Psychiatric Hospital and Residential Institution (1991) https://www.parliament.vic.gov.au/papers/govpub/VPARL1988-92No198.pdf.

VPRS 18303. Register of Complaints Against Staff. 1871–1948.

VPRS 18137. Seclusion Register 1869–1881 Ararart Asylum for the Insane.

Waldron, David. *The sign of the Witch: Modernity and the Pagan Revival.* Carolina Academic Press, 2008.

Walter, B. S. G. (2014) 'Listening to ghosts: Haunted hospitals, spectral patients, and the monstrous in modern medicine'. *Trespassing Medicine, 4*, 51–2.

Wang, J. '13,000 deaths in 130 years: Ararat Lunatic Asylum is the most haunted place in Australia', https://www.mamamia.com.au/ararat-mental-asylum-australias-haunted-building/.

Westmore, A. (2008) 'Eric Cunningham Dax (1908–2008): A Tribute', *Journal of Health and History*, Vol. 10 No. 1, Australian and New Zealand Society of the History of Medicine.

Williams, J. (1952) 'Psychiatric Facts and Fictions', *Medical Journal of Australia* Vol. 1.2

Willis, Elizabeth. (1999) '... of "unsound mind"', *Historic Environment*, 14(2), 33–8.

Wright, D. (1997) 'Getting out of the asylum: understanding the confinement of the insane in the nineteenth century'. *Social History of Medicine*, 10(1), 137–55.

Zerubavel, E. (1996) 'Social Memories: Steps to a sociology of the past.' *Qualitative Sociology*, 19(3), 283–99.

Print Media

The Age

Ararat Advertiser

Argus

Ballarat Star

Bendigo Advertiser

Geelong Advertiser

Herald Sun

Illustrated Post

Mount Alexander Mail

Port Phillip Gazette

Port Phillip Patriot and Morning Advertiser

Sydney Gazette

Sydney Morning Herald

York Press

Television and Cinema

Aradale Lunatic Asylum. *Haunting Australia*. Season 1, Episode 3, https://www.imdb.com/title/tt3526418/.

Aradale Psychiatric Hospital. *Mystical Guides: Haunted Australia*. Season 1, Episode 3, https://www.imdb.com/title/tt4928516/locations.

Tujuh Bidadari, https://www.imdb.com/title/tt9160672/.

The Devils Backbone, https://www.imdb.com/title/tt0256009/.

Index

About the Authors

Dr David Waldron is a Senior Lecturer in History at Federation University Australia with a research focus on folklore and community heritage. He is the author of *Sign of the Witch: Modernity and the Pagan Revival* (Carolina Academic Press, 2008), *Shock! The Black Dog of Bungay – a Case Study in Local Folklore* (Hidden Press, 2010) and *Snarls from the Tea-Tree: Victoria's Big Cat Folklore* (Australian Scholarly Publishing, 2013) and editor/contributor of *Goldfields and the Gothic: A Hidden Heritage and Folklore* (Australian Scholarly Publishing, 2016). He is regularly involved in public engagements, festivals and multi-media displays including Ballarat Heritage Weekend and is the co-writer and researcher for the National Trust Australia People's Choice award historical pod cast series 'Tales from Rat City'.

Sharn Waldron is a member of the UK Council for Psychotherapy (UKCP) via the Association of Jungian Analysts, a registered Psychoanalyst with the Australian New Zealand Association of Psychotherapists (ANZAP) and has international accreditation through the International Association of of Analytical Psychotherapists. She is a registered Jungian analyst and supervisor. She lives and works in Geelong, Australia, and has trained in family therapy, couples' therapy, and in work with individuals. She has worked as a psychotherapist in industry, the military, community health, community services, as well as in private practice. Holding a master of arts in Psychoanalytic Studies from La Trobe University, Melbourne, she has written articles and papers for the National Health Trust Association (UK), *Pears Cyclopaedia* (Penguin Books), *The Australian Journal of Psychotherapy,*

Mantis (South Africa), *Quadrant* (New York), *Folklore* (UK), Australian Scholarly Publishing, *Review de Psychologie Analytique*, *The Journal of Analytical Psychology* (UK), and *Jung Journal of Culture and Psyche.*

Nathaniel Buchanan is passionate researcher of Dark History and manager of Eerie Tours which operates at the former Ararat Lunatic Asylum. He graduated from the University of Queensland with an honours in History and a degree in Teaching before securing a position as a tour manager for Contiki Tours Europe, where he studied the intricacies of tour guiding and storytelling. Following this, he worked for several ghost and dark history tour companies in Europe before heading back to Australia to live on site at the infamous Port Arthur. He moved to Ballarat in 2008 to create Eerie Tours, which includes ghost and cemetery tours in Ballarat and surrounding towns. He began Aradale Ghost Tours in 2010 and was awarded a Victorian Tourism Award in the Cultural Tourism category in 2017 for his contributions to Dark Tourism in the state.

www.ingramcontent.com/pod-product-compliance
Ingram Content Group Australia Pty Ltd
76 Discovery Rd, Dandenong South VIC 3175, AU
AUHW020910070726
429584AU00004B/45

9 781925 984910